P9-CCU-503

THE SOUTHERN WRITER

IN THE

POSTMODERN WORLD

■

MERCER UNIVERSITY LAMAR MEMORIAL LECTURES NO. 33

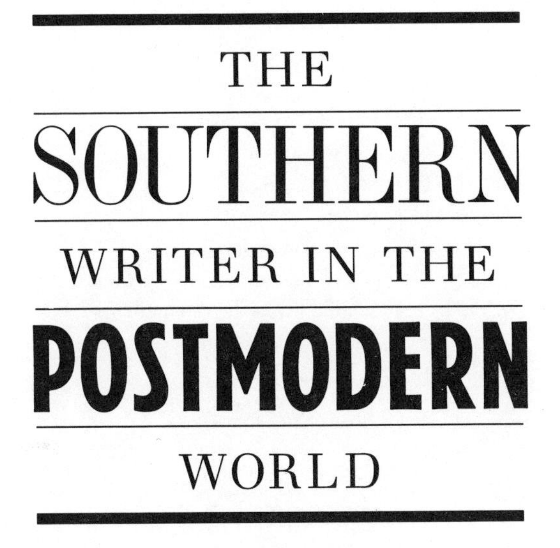

Fred Hobson

THE UNIVERSITY OF GEORGIA PRESS / ATHENS & LONDON

128865

© 1991 by the University of Georgia Press
Athens, Georgia 30602
All rights reserved
Designed by Louise M. Jones
Set in 10/14 Linotype Walbaum
The paper in this book meets the guidelines for permanence and durability of the Committee on Production Guidelines for Book Longevity of the Council on Library Resources.

Printed in the United States of America

95 94 93 92 91 5 4 3 2 1

Library of Congress Cataloging in Publication Data
Hobson, Fred C., date.
The southern writer in the postmodern world / Fred Hobson. p. cm. — (Mercer University Lamar memorial lectures ; no. 33)
Includes bibliographical references (p.) and index.
ISBN 0-8203-1275-4 (alk. paper)
1. American literature—Southern States—History and criticism. 2. American literature—20th century—History and criticism. 3. Postmodernism (Literature)—Southern States. 4. Southern States—Intellectual life—1865– . 5. Southern States in literature. I. Title. II. Series: Lamar memorial lectures ; no. 33.
PS261.H535 1991 813'.5409975—dc20
90-11031 CIP

British Library Cataloging in Publication Data available

For
Louis D. Rubin, Jr.
and
Lewis P. Simpson

Contents

■

Foreword

■

In this volume drawn from the thirty-third series of Lamar Memorial Lectures, Professor Fred Hobson of the University of North Carolina ventures readings of the most recent southern fiction, the works composed by what seems to be a third or even fourth generation of the Southern Renascence. These younger writers, fifty and under, grew up during or after the civil rights movement of the sixties, a time that was as pivotal in southern life and letters as the twenties had been for earlier generations.

The younger writers are not writing with the "burden" of racial guilt; they are writing about "unburdened" characters who are very different at first glance from Quentin Compson and Jack Burden and their brothers and sisters in classic Renascence fiction. Recent novels still feature distinctively southern voices, but their characters apparently do not have the southern-consciousness and self-consciousness typical of a Faulkner character.

The lives of these characters, immersed in the American mass culture, may seem emptier and flatter, but Professor Hobson finds more in the novels of Bobbie Ann Mason and Richard Ford than first meets the eye. He shows us that "minimalist" fiction may be read better by the "non-minimalist reader" (Professor Hobson's memorable phrase from the first lecture) and that such novels may be concerned in their own way about several of the subjects that concern the characters of Faulkner, Warren, and Percy: history, the past, and the "ambiguous afflictions" consequent to internecine warfare.

Professor Hobson also demonstrates in the representative cases of Ernest Gaines and Fred Chappell a kind of writing which, while set in the contemporary South, is in some respects more clearly attuned to the "autochthonous ideal" of the Agrarians. He argues impressively that Gaines is the contemporary writer whose work best fits the standards that the Renascence gave us.

Fred Hobson has become the leader of his generation of critics who study southern literature and culture. The Lamar Lectures committee is grateful to him both for the excellence of his lectures and for their subject and their timing: he has brought the Lectures full circle, helping to begin a new generation of Lamar Lectures, which are moving to the study of more recent phenomena as they continue Mrs. Lamar's desire "to provide lectures of the very highest type of scholarship that will aid in the permanent preservation of southern culture, history, and literature."

Michael M. Cass
for the Lamar Memorial Lectures Committee

Preface

■

These remarks on contemporary southern fiction are an expanded version of the Lamar Memorial Lectures delivered at Mercer University in October 1989. What they consist of is not rigorous scholarship so much as a trying out of ideas, a preliminary estimate of writing going on around us in the South. The value of the Lamar Lectures, it seems to me, is precisely this: they allow a scholar to undertake a subject about which he or she has *something* to say but not enough to fill a three-hundred-page book—a subject he would like to explore, would like to venture certain opinions on, but concerning which he has no intention of pronouncing the final word. Such is particularly the case when one is dealing with novelists who are in their thirties, forties, and fifties, and who will undergo any number of transitions and transformations before they complete their careers.

I would like to say that I have enjoyed writing this book perhaps more than any other I have undertaken, and the reason lies largely in the freedom given the Lamar lecturer by the Lamar Committee at Mercer University. I would like to go on record as well in saying that the reputation of the Lamar Committee for splendid hospitality is well deserved. I wish to thank, in particular, Professor Wayne Mixon, chair of the committee, whose wide and deep knowledge of the American South, its history and its literature, would probably qualify him to give these lectures himself each year. Wayne and Fran Mixon were the most gracious and most generous of hosts. I am also grateful to Michael and Lynn Cass and Henry and Pat Warnock for their gracious hospitality. Aside from these and other persons connected with Mercer University, I acknowledge the following debts: to Frances Coombs, who typed the cleanest manuscript—out of the untidiest final draft—I have ever seen; to Malcolm Call, Karen Orchard, Debra Winter, and Ellen Harris of the University of Georgia Press; and especially, in the writing of this book, to the members of my seminar in contemporary southern literature at Louisiana State University in the spring of 1989—particularly to Edward Dupuy, Michael Griffith, and John Zmirak—and to Ann Henley, whose knowledge of southern fiction is surpassed only by her knowledge of most other fiction written in English. These scholars—as well as accomplished South-watchers Louis D. Rubin, Jr., Lewis P. Simpson, Julius Rowan Raper, Jane Hobson, and Linda Whitney Hobson—contributed greatly to my understanding of the mind and expression of the contemporary South.

THE SOUTHERN WRITER IN THE POSTMODERN WORLD

■

1

The Contemporary Southern Writer and the Tradition

Some thirty years ago Donald Davidson of Vanderbilt University gave to the inaugural series of the Lamar Lectures the title *Southern Writers in the Modern World.* In those lectures the Southern Agrarian Davidson was interested in the role of the writer in a radically changing world: the South of the 1920s, and the response of the Fugitive-Agrarians to it, was his particular interest.[1] I do not share a great deal with Davidson as far as his view of the South is concerned, but I do share his interest in what happens to the southern writer as the South changes, as conditions that gave rise to earlier writers seem not to be with us any more. The world I wish to discuss here is the contemporary South, and the writers I have in mind are principally (although not exclusively) those who began to write during or after the 1960s—and in some cases not until the 1980s.

I am particularly interested in the continuity—or lack of continuity—between certain attitudes, assumptions, and even values that informed southern literature during its first great flowering, the Southern Renascence of the 1920s, 1930s, 1940s, and, we might add, 1950s. During the years of the Renascence it was assumed—and accepted by all, friend and foe—that the South was the defeated, failed, poor, unprogressive part of the United States. But an irony of southern literary history, to go along with all the other southern ironies, is that this legacy of defeat and failure served well the writer in the South. Like Quentin Compson at Harvard, the southern writer wore his heritage of failure and defeat—and often guilt—as his badge of honor. It provided him or her something that no other American writer, or at least American novelist, of the twentieth century had in any abundance—that is, a tragic sense. The Southerner alone among Americans, as C. Vann Woodward has pointed out, had known defeat, had known what it was not to succeed, not to prosper. The Southerner, that is, shared with the rest of the world, but not with the nonsouthern parts of the United States, the realization that things do not always work out. The southern writer, thus, was born with a knowledge—or soon acquired it—that the nonsouthern American writer did not have, at least in his inherited historical consciousness. Just as failure is more interesting than success (particularly failure when so much was hoped and expected) and defeat more interesting than victory, the southern writer had a great advantage over his nonsouthern counterpart. As Quentin said to Shreve McCannon at Harvard, "You would have to be born there."[2] Whether, in all cases, you *would* have to be born there is beside the point. The southern writer believed you did. Much that was southern helped to contribute to a tragic sense.

Not to mention high drama. As Richard Weaver wrote in his essay "Aspects of the Southern Philosophy": "The fact is simply that for the North the South is too theatrical to be wholly real." Or, to draw again on *Absalom, Absalom!*, this time Shreve to Quentin on the South, "It's better than *Ben Hur*" (p. 217). The South *was* dramatic. If racial tension, conflict, violence—as well as unrealistic but lofty aspirations—made for tragedy, they also made for spectacle; the Gothic South in *general* made for spectacle. It is a wonder that the southern writer did not seize his advantage before the 1920s, the late 1920s at that. Exactly what happened in that decade, of course, has been documented and discussed by any number of writers and scholars, most prominently Allen Tate and Louis D. Rubin, Jr.: the southern writer, who in most cases had left home for a time, focused his eye on a changing South, an industrializing South, but looked as well at a South that was slipping away, and the result was a creative mixture of detachment and involvement—an escape from, then an attempt to return to the southern community—that contributed greatly to the work of Faulkner and Wolfe and the Southern Agrarians.[3]

One found numerous attempts in the 1930s, 1940s, and 1950s to define, to describe, the Southern Temper, the Southern Mind, and one still finds them. The attempts came largely, although not exclusively, from the Southern Agrarians and certain neo-Agrarians such as Richard Weaver,[4] and one feels in part that these attempts were, among other things, efforts to capture the Southerner, to define him or her (and, one feels, in most cases, *him*) before he slipped away. Some of these "aspects of the southern philosophy" identified and celebrated by the Agrarians and neo-Agrarians are open to debate, although others are less so. One might say with some certainty that those qualities stemming at least in part from the Civil War and its aftermath—a greater attention to the past, an acceptance of man's finiteness, his penchant for failure, a tragic sense—*are* more characteristic of the Southerner than of other Americans; but certain other qualities that are indeed representatively southern—a religious sense, a closeness to nature, a great attention to and affection for place, a close attention to family, a preference for the concrete and a rage against abstraction—might also be said to be rather characteristic of any rural people who have lived in a traditional society in a single area for a great number of years: upper New England, north of Boston, for example, or even parts of the eastern Middle West. In fact, as concerns the presumed southern preference for concreteness, one might contend that the southern mind, despite its stated abhorrence of abstraction from the 1840s on, has been in certain respects the most abstract of minds. No American writer was more given to those abstractions honor and duty —to the whole code of chivalry and to other codes that ordered and prescribed behavior—than Thomas Nelson Page. One could also easily contend that the Civil War was fought, in part, over an abstraction, the extension of slavery into western territory that could not have supported slavery in any case. But to Southerners it was a matter of principle—and an insult to southern pride. And in later southern society, what else was racial segregation but a monstrous abstraction, what else but an abstraction the identifying and categorizing (and thus restricting) of any individuals—blacks and women in particular—by group?

But, these questions aside, I think it can be said that the most notable southern *writers*, white and black, of the 1920s, 1930s, and 1940s were far more conscious of place, family, community, religion and its social manifestations, and the power of the past in the present than were nonsouthern American writers, and that southern *writers* did rage against abstraction more than nonsouthern writers. (Certainly Hemingway wars against abstraction in *A Farewell to Arms*, but not nearly so much as Faulkner and Flannery O'Connor in much of their fiction—not to mention southern polemicists such as Davidson who railed in numerous essays against abstraction, sociology, social planning, and various social and cultural indexes which put southern states at the bottom.) So did those southern writers of the 1950s and most of the 1960s concern themselves with place, family, community, and religion. In particular the southern writer of that latter period continued to be fascinated with history, with the southern past and the individual past as it was involved with the regional past. And the southern writer through the 1960s seemed very much aware, as well, of those *writers* who had gone before. Most notable southern novelists through the 1960s, it seems to me, still wrote with an eye very much on past southern giants. William Styron, one of the two or three most significant southern novelists of the past forty years, could not seem to escape, did not seem to *want* to escape, the influence of Faulkner and Wolfe. In ways that have been pointed out by Louis Rubin and others, *Lie Down in Darkness* was *The Sound and the Fury* cast in Tidewater Virginia.[5] One also had to be reminded of Faulkner, although less obviously, in *The Confessions of Nat Turner*. And in *Sophie's Choice*, a novel written in the 1970s but belonging very much to the 1950s and 1960s, Styron seemed in many ways to be rewriting Thomas Wolfe. Stingo, the autobiographical protagonist of a long, wordy, self-indulgent novel—another young, impressionable, oversexed WASP up from college in the North Carolina Piedmont, finding a place in Brooklyn, fascinated by the man-swarm of New York, particularly fascinated by Jewishness and ethnicity, and out to write the Great American Novel—*is* in many ways the young Thomas Wolfe or Eugene Gant or George Webber. Styron could leave Wolfe behind no more easily than he could leave Faulkner, and, again, he did not really seem to want to.

Nor could any number of writers as late as the 1960s relinquish one of the southern writer's traditional roles in relation to his society, which was in many, although not all, cases an adversary relationship, or more accurately a love-hate relationship seen in numerous earlier writers but exemplified best by a tortured fictional character, Quentin, in *Absalom, Absalom!* Shame, guilt, anger, pride: these were still the feelings pronounced by many southern writers of the 1960s, seen both in novels dealing with race and the civil rights movement and perhaps even more dramatically in a number of nonfiction works of contrition and confession, Willie Morris's *North Toward Home* and Larry King's *Confessions of a White Racist*, among others. These two books, as I have discussed elsewhere, were very much in the tradition of

George Washington Cable, W. J. Cash, and Lillian Smith, among white writers—and, in a different way, Richard Wright, among black writers—a tradition which required that the writer probe deeply and painfully his relationship to his homeland. But something seemed to be missing in these latter-day confessionals. They are interesting and eloquent—*North Toward Home* has become, deservedly, something of a southern classic—but one wonders if their authors really *meant* it as deeply as Cable and Cash and Smith, and especially Wright, had, if they were risking all in their truth-telling as their predecessors had. Or were they merely writing in a particularly southern mode, writing the obligatory love-hate memoir more out of custom and habit, and the realization that they had a good story to tell, than out of true rage, fear, guilt, or shame? In the South of the late 1960s positive thinking, not contrition, was dominant. Could the writer in *that* South write with the same intensity and conviction that drove Cable and Smith and Cash—or, in a different way, Faulkner? Had what was once natural become stylized, what was deeply and painfully experienced become ritualized?

To some extent I believe it had, but one quality which much of the writing through the early 1970s did share with the writing that had gone before was an acute self-consciousness, an intense awareness of *being* southern, as well as a preoccupation with old themes, old settings and truisms. Many white southern writers, generally speaking, still thought they had a love-hate relationship with the South whether they did or not, and those writers had to write the traditional work coming to terms with their homeland.

I do not believe that is the case with most white southern writers who have begun to publish in the past fifteen or twenty years. Those writers—again, broadly speaking—seem hardly to have the need to join the battle, to wrestle with racial sin and guilt. What one finds in more recent novelists such as Bobbie Ann Mason and Anne Tyler is a relative *lack* of southern self-consciousness. This is not to say that the *voice* often isn't southern; with writers such as Lee Smith and Clyde Edgerton it certainly is. And especially it is not to contend that black southern writers—one thinks of Ernest Gaines, Alice Walker, and James Alan McPherson—have forgotten the pain and suffering in the South before 1965 and some of the pain that endures. Nor, finally, can one contend that, among white writers, the earlier benighted South of fiction—what Gerald W. Johnson after reading Faulkner and Caldwell in 1935 called the Raw-Head-and-Bloody-Bones school of southern fiction[6]—has been left behind completely. Cormac McCarthy, Harry Crews, and Barry Hannah, among other novelists, write a sort of neo-Southern Gothic. McCarthy's *Child of God* (1973), a tale of murder and necrophilia more lurid than anything Faulkner or Caldwell ever invented—or, in a more contemporary vein, Hannah's *Ray* (1980)—assure us that a Gothic South still lives in imaginative literature. The problem for the neo-Gothic novelist is that southern social reality, broad and representative reality, no longer so dramatically supports his fiction.

And with a change in that social reality, and the perception of that change, has come a somewhat different set of assumptions among southern writers. It was in the late 1960s that perceptions and assumptions began to change radically. The decade of the sixties, in fact, might be seen as pivotal in southern life and letters in much the same way the 1920s was: it was a time of numerous southern crimes against humanity, of notable attention and criticism from without, of great intellectual ferment. The scenes this time were Birmingham and Selma and Philadelphia, Mississippi—not Dayton, Tennessee, and Gastonia—but the effect was the same: southern barbarism was exposed, southern traditions and mores were challenged, the South changed (although more decisively this time), a watershed in southern thought resulted—and, in some ways, a new southern fiction emerged. The new set of assumptions had something to do with the fact that, after the 1960s, it appeared that the South had endured its crisis, had triumphed over itself, had in fact come through. It had—at least so said the self-congratulators—thrown off the old albatross of segregation, and with that presumably gone, and with Sun Belt prosperity coming, the South seemed no longer the defeated, failed, poor, guilt-ridden, tragic part of America. What that change meant to the southern writer is intriguing. Faulkner and the great fiction writers of the Renascence had written, as we have seen, with the assumption that the South *was* defeated, guilt-ridden, backward-looking, and tragic: much of the power of their fiction came from that assumption. What was the writer of the seventies and eighties to do with a suddenly Superior South, optimistic, forward-looking, more virtuous and now threatening to become more prosperous than the rest of the country? Success would require a new voice—and less reliance on the models of the past.

Certainly that voice did not emerge all at once, was rarely seen in fact before the 1970s, although Walker Percy was in many ways writing a new fiction before that time. But since the 1970s that new voice—or those voices—are hard to miss, and what I propose to do here is to discuss some of those voices and examine the extent to which, broadly speaking, recent writers have shared (or not shared) those concerns with place, family, community, religion, and the past which have been central in the most notable southern fiction of the first three-quarters of this century.

First I should explain what I mean by "recent voices," since many voices of thirty or forty years ago are still being heard. What I mean, essentially, is those writers under forty-five or fifty who were born during or since the Second World War and came of age in the 1950s and 1960s, what one might call the third generation of modern southern literature—although in my concluding remarks I shall draw on certain earlier writers. What is evident in any discussion is that these writers have various and conflicting attitudes toward the South and the contemporary world—for there are as many "treatments" of place, family, community, and so forth as there are individual southern writers—and thus this discussion will rely at first on certain generalizations. To begin with, as the title of this volume suggests, the contemporary southern writer, like the contemporary American writer, lives in a postmodern world, a world in which order, structure, and meaning—including narrative order, structure, and meaning—are constantly called into question. As Julius Rowan Raper has argued, however, the southern writer in a postmodern world is not necessarily, is not usually, a postmodern *writer*.[7] That is to say, the contemporary southern writer—with the exception of John Barth and, on occasion, writers such as Barry Hannah, Richard Ford, and James Alan McPherson—essentially *accepts*, rather than invents, his world, is not given to fantasy, does not *in his fiction* question the whole assumed relationship between narrator and narrative, does not question the nature of fiction itself. The contemporary southern fiction writer, although he or she may experiment with time sequence and point of view (as the great southern modernist Faulkner did, after all), in more basic respects usually plays by the old rules of the game.

Certain other generalizations inform these remarks. First, most recent southern writers *seem*, at least at first glance, to be comparatively devoid of influence from past southern literary giants, and certainly are now out of the shadow of Faulkner. If there is any shadow they operate within (and such a conclusion I reach not only in considering some of the best fiction that has been published in the South in the past fifteen years but also from having looked at a couple of thousand manuscripts which came across the desk of the *Southern Review* in the late 1980s), it is that of Eudora Welty and, to a lesser extent, Flannery O'Connor and Walker Percy, not Faulkner. A second generalization: it might be said that most of the writers I am talking about

—Bobbie Ann Mason, Josephine Humphreys, Lee Smith, Barry Hannah, Richard Ford, Jayne Anne Phillips, Clyde Edgerton, and Jill McCorkle, to name several—immerse their characters in a world of popular or mass culture, and their characters' perceptions of place, family, community, and even myth are greatly conditioned by popular culture, television, movies, rock music, and so forth. And finally, few of those under-fifty writers attempt to write the "big novel" in the manner of Faulkner and Wolfe, Warren and Styron—or, to name a contemporary black nonsouthern (or half-southern) novelist, Toni Morrison. Indeed, if one has any concern at all about the very healthy condition of contemporary southern fiction, it might be that one sometimes finds—despite an abundance of literary skill, verisimilitude, charm, picturesqueness, and humor—a relative want of *power*, a power that often had its origins in or at least was related to—in Warren, Styron, and part of Faulkner—a certain southern self-consciousness; a power that, in Warren and Styron, stemmed in part from a philosophical, even mildly didactic intent, the kind of writing associated with the novel of ideas, the novel of historical meditation, or the novel concerned with sweeping social change. I say this while realizing that I am perhaps looking for a particular *kind* of power, a particular sort of "ambitious novel." The work of Mason, Smith, Edgerton, and numerous other writers possesses the power of observation, the energy and vitality of life as lived, the power of telling the truth (concrete, tangible small truths of the kind associated with Welty's fiction), and that is no small accomplishment.

But enough of generalizations. If I am to be approximately in a southern tradition—concrete, not abstract—let me in the remarks that follow turn to particular writers, particular stories.

2

A Question of Culture—and History: Bobbie Ann Mason, Lee Smith, and Barry Hannah

I want to begin by examining the impact of mass or commercial, popular culture on contemporary southern fiction because we find here one of the great departures from the work of the past. This is not to say that earlier writers ignored *their* popular cultures altogether. Celebrities and brand names abound in a story such as Welty's "Why I Live at the P.O.," and Faulkner gave characters names drawn from *his* accessible popular culture—Montgomery Ward Snopes, Watkins Products Snopes, and Wallstreet Panic Snopes. But such inventions for Faulkner were partly for his own amusement, partly commentary on lives devoid of tradition and family identity. Now, in part because of its pervasiveness, its powerful influence, we must take mass culture much more seriously. One finds, because of popular culture, new twists on old concerns and preoccupations, new ways of perceiving. It is not enough to simply dismiss all this as K-Mart Realism, or its even poorer country cousin, the wondrously named Grit Lit.

The writer identified most closely with a world whose boundaries are the twenty-three inches of a television screen or the parking lot of one's nearest mall is Bobbie Ann Mason, author of a critically acclaimed collection of stories, *Shiloh* (1982), as well as two novels, the highly successful *In Country* (1985) and *Spence + Lila* (1988). In Mason's fiction, particularly the first two volumes, one finds characters forever riding a wave of popular culture, popular music and television programs in particular, wherever it takes them, deriving their values, their mythology, even their sense of time and family and community, their *identity*, from shared rock stars and television programs. Family to seventeen-year-old Sam in *In Country* is Hawkeye and Colonel Blake and the other characters on *M*A*S*H*, and community is those other people out there who also see and believe in *M*A*S*H*. Time periods—seasons—find their reference not, as they traditionally have, in terms of natural calamity or moments of historical import; rather, as Mason begins part 2 of *In Country*, "It was the summer of the Michael Jackson *Victory* tour and the Bruce Springsteen *Born in the U.S.A.* tour."[1]

Mason is generally included among those writers who are said to write "minimalist" fiction, and that term—suggesting a fiction that focuses on everyday concerns of rather average people with no great sense of self, a fiction that presents, rather drily and matter-of-factly, a slice of often depressing life—certainly applies to the stories in *Shiloh*, if not altogether to Mason's novels. Minimalist fiction is a natural outgrowth of late twentieth-century minimalist American life, in which little is risked or even attempted, little expected (it may have certain antecedents in Hemingway's fiction or, before that, in literary naturalism), but it appears at first glance particularly out of place in the American South whose writers have those words of Faulkner—"love and honor and pity and pride and compassion and sacrifice"; or "man will not merely endure: he will prevail"[2]—ringing in their ears. For the most notable southern fiction of the twentieth century, as indeed even the least notable of the nineteenth, has been characterized by a certain elevated sense, a sense—as we have observed —of living dramatically, tied both to language and to certain notions about grandeur of person and nobility of purpose, and sometimes both.

Mason has, almost defiantly, none of those notions: in *Shiloh* she is unpretentious with a vengeance. If it is said of Henry James that none of his characters have to work, it might be said of Mason that *all* of her characters have to work, and nearly all at menial tasks. But we are struck not so much by economic poverty in her characters—economics is really of little importance to her—but rather emotional and spiritual poverty. One finds in the *Shiloh* stories nearly a complete absence of nurturing family, community, and religion, those staples of traditional southern life and literature. Some of the inhabitants of the small towns in Mason's western Kentucky give up; most just absorb disappointment and carry on with gritty determination, finding some temporary pleasure in the mass culture around them.

Most of the characters in the *Shiloh* stories are in their thirties and forties; the protagonist of *In Country* is seventeen, but her life, as she grows older, will almost certainly be theirs. The world of Samantha Hughes, even more than theirs, is a world contained within the borders of popular or commercial culture. It would be difficult, in fact, to find *any* character in any fiction so much a product of that world, and few characters so devoid of a traditional sense of place. The epigraph to the novel, from Bruce Springsteen's "Born in the U.S.A.," is well chosen:

> *I'm ten years burning down the road*
> *Nowhere to run ain't got nowhere to go.*

The road *is* place, and as Sam, her Vietnam-veteran uncle, Emmett, and her grandmother drive from the ironically named Hopewell, Kentucky, to Washington to find Sam's father's name on the Vietnam memorial, every place along the way is equally home. "Sam loves the room," Mason writes as they stop at a Howard Johnson's the first night. "The room is so clean, with no evidence of belonging to anybody" (pp. 11–12). No place is foreign as long as it has television. "Johnny Carson has Joan Rivers substituting," Emmett announces the next night (p. 19). ("It's a rerun," he complains, and—as if to further convince those who contend there is no irony in Mason—he adds, "Nothing's authentic anymore.") Television, as we have said, is family, or the nearest Sam can come to family since her father is dead, her mother living in another city, and her uncle, who lives with her, shattered by his experience in Vietnam. Carson and Ed McMahon are a couple of uncles, Rivers the unfavorite aunt. *M*A*S*H* completes the family: "Years ago, when Colonel Blake was killed, Sam was so shocked she went around stunned for days. She was only a child then, and his death on the program was more real to her than the death of her own father" (p. 25). Sam's responses to life, her assumptions about human behavior, are taken from television as well. Near the end, as Emmett comes as close as he ever will to confronting the horrors of Vietnam, Sam "thought he was going to come out with some suppressed memories of events as dramatic as that one that caused Hawkeye to crack up in the final episode of *M*A*S*H.* But nothing came" (p. 222). Later, when he does tell her about a time he almost died, she responds, "That sounds familiar. I saw something like that in a movie on TV." "I know the one you're thinking about," Emmett says. "This was completely different. It really happened" (p. 223). Television isn't life, Sam at last realizes. After Emmett breaks down, sobbing, she transcends popular culture for one of the few times in the novel: "She resisted the temptation to turn on the car radio" (p. 244).

What Mason writes, of course, is not new. Tom Sawyer and Henry Fleming, in nineteenth-century American fiction, were nearly as much products and prisoners of *their* popular culture —largely romantic books and the popular press—as Sam is of hers; and Emmett, at least until he breaks down, resembles the scarred Hemingway war veteran, the survivor taking pleasure in doing small things well and trying to forget the past. Nearly all the characters in *In Country*, indeed, are trying to forget. "I can't live in the past," Sam's mother tells her. "It was all such a stupid waste. There's nothing to remember" (p. 168). "I don't go around stirring up trouble," says a Vietnam friend of Emmett. "Sure, I've got memories, but I've learned responsibility" (p. 113). And the past is no guide to the present. "You can't learn from the past," Emmett insists. "The main thing you learn from history is that you can't learn from history. That's what history is" (p. 226).

Such were hardly the sentiments of those earlier fictional Southerners Quentin Compson and Jack Burden, who were obsessed by history; of Allen Tate, who wrote about the power of the past in the present; or of William Faulkner, whose Gavin Stevens insisted that for him the past was not dead, it wasn't even past.[3] If Faulkner, Warren, Ellison, Styron—indeed nearly all the notable southern writers of fiction save Welty—have had a common preoccupation, it *is* history, particularly southern history, and Mason would seem to inhabit an altogether different fictional world. But, in its way, *In Country* is a novel very much concerned with history, and Sam a character nearly as single-minded as Quentin Compson and Jack Burden in her attempts to unlock secrets of the past. It is just that history, to Sam, goes back no further than the mid-1960s and the Vietnam War, and that *her* historical search is a very private search since her father died in that war.

This is a southern novel about a war, then, a lost war and a truly lost cause, and that kind of novel is hardly new on the southern scene. This is a war a full century after Appomattox, yet in encountering *In Country* the reader with a historical sense finds it difficult to ignore that earlier war altogether. There are no explicit references to the Civil War, except on one occasion to "Civil War stuff" hanging on people's walls (which leads Sam to wonder [p. 80] when people will "start putting M-16s and pictures of missiles on their living room walls"), yet one finds, ten or fifteen years after Vietnam, as after the Civil War, an intense period of questioning, an asking what went wrong. Moreover, Sam, no less than Thomas Nelson Page's characters, looks back to a halcyon period "before the war"—for Sam that means the early 1960s when the Beatles first came to America—and if her knowledge of the period *ante bellum* is flawed or nearly nonexistent, is that really so different from those ex-Confederates who looked back on an earlier South? Indeed, Sam's search for meaning is, in most respects, a more honest search than theirs, her obsession a far more respectable one, for it takes the form of a search for truth, not justification. Sam *wants* to understand in a way many of the ex-Confederates—at least most of those whose writing has reached us—really did not, and she is able to acknowledge (even without understanding fully) that the American cause in Vietnam was flawed—something the post–Civil War southern apologists, who never admitted how truly lost was the southern cause, how truly unworthy and doomed from the beginning, rarely could bring themselves to do. Both the South of 1860 and America of 1960 had, in their innocence, believed themselves a chosen people, and in each case defeat was a profound shock that drove the losers to wonder why. The ex-Confederates (particularly the Presbyterian divines among them) turned to their Bibles for theological answers, Sam to more secular sources—books on Vietnam, accounts of veterans, and her father's diary. She did not have the consolation of those earlier Southerners who believed, who *willed* themselves to believe, that, despite defeat, God was and remained on their side.[4]

In still other ways, of course, America after Vietnam differed spiritually and emotionally from the South after Appomattox. One finds, in the *1980s*, few monuments glorifying this latest lost cause, but rather a single monument, the Vietnam memorial, and in it one finds not glory but collective guilt. As Sam's grandmother says, at the end, while looking into the shiny blackness of the memorial, "All I can see here is my reflection" (p. 244). Similarly, the reunion of Vietnam vets Mason pictures—a veterans' dance, with a table displaying snapshots of soldiers, plastic weapons, and planes—is nearly a parody of those celebratory gatherings Confederate veterans had begun to stage by the early 1880s. These Vietnam vets appear not with missing arms and legs (although such soldiers could have been found) but rather with suspicions, though not the certainty, that their health has been ruined by Agent Orange—an ambiguous affliction after an ambiguous war. The veterans' dance is as close as one comes in *In Country* to a sense of community: the veterans *are* a community grounded in shared experiences and frustrations, but a community nearly fragmented. Unlike the ex-Confederates, they have no devotion to, no absorption in a cause, no desire to relive, to recapture what they have been through. The vets argue, they fight, they can view what they have been through neither tragically (which would have brought a certain cleansing) nor even ironically (which would at least bring a certain intellectual satisfaction). There was indeed irony in Vietnam, but Mason's vets are in no position to appreciate it, and America as a nation would have to wait somewhat longer after Vietnam to learn fully the lesson that the South (though, in *its* case, not fully until the twentieth century) learned from the Civil War—that defeat brings those, once isolated by pride or success, into a full awareness of the human condition, the universal experience. Such ideas would have been lofty, abstract, and far away for the veterans at Mason's dance. They could take little comfort in helping to initiate America into the condition, sooner or later, of all people.

In Country, then, is a novel about history in which none of the characters has any interest in history, save Sam in her immediate desire to know her father and the war in which he died. Otherwise, Sam is a point-of-view character to whom all is of nearly equal significance—Colonel Blake's death on *M*A*S*H*, her father's death, Hawkeye's crack-up—so connected are her points of reference, her mythology, to mass culture, to an artificial rendering of experience. As admirable as Sam's brief search for historical truth is, it goes no further than Vietnam. A deeper knowledge of history—*before* Vietnam—would help *explain* Vietnam. A deeper knowledge on the part of the right people at the right time—of American leaders in the late 1950s and early 1960s—might have prevented Vietnam, might have prevented her father's death. One of the novel's fine ironies is contained in Emmett's statement, "You can't learn from history": if we had learned from history early enough, he would not be the physical and emotional wreck the war made of him.

This, of course, argues for the importance of history on purely utilitarian grounds—one can argue on the same grounds for the importance of historical knowledge in any matter involving a democratic state—and it is far from elitist, I believe, to argue further that Mason's characters also live lives less full and rich than is possible because of an ignorance of and lack of interest in the historical past, because they have little in their world to make life meaningful beyond the here-and-now. (Religion—a spiritual commitment of some kind—might offer a similar transcendence, but that is harder to come by.) Thus, what we have here are characters who inhabit shopping malls and drive-ins with no idea of and no concern for what was there fifty years before, no idea of how they fit into the whole picture, temporally or spatially. And Sam and Emmett can hardly be blamed: they lack the tools—the incentive, the example—to dig any deeper because they are products of a *society* that disregards history.

What does this say about Mason's responsibility as a novelist? She is writing fiction, after all—dramatizing individual lives—not writing history or commentary on history, and if Sam Hughes, rather than Jack Burden, is Mason's point-of-view character, we can hardly complain. It is radically unfair to expect her, in undertaking a novel on Vietnam and its aftermath, to write the novel Robert Penn Warren or William Styron might have written. Nothing compels her to be the moralist, the novelist of ideas, they (particularly Warren) often are. Moreover, we should not commit that old critical sin of identifying the novelist too closely with her point-of-view character. In fact, Mason, in her way, does value history, even offers a meditation on history.[5]

So this is not to say that Mason has no interest in history; but it is to contend that, in many respects, minimalism and history do not mix well. Or, to put it another way, minimalist fiction requires a nonminimalist reader, and that has probably been the case since Hemingway. In *In Country*, for example, one finds no meaningful corrective—rhetorical, dramatic, or metaphorical—to Emmett's statement "You can't learn from history." The reader himself or herself must bring *to* the novel the knowledge that provides such a corrective, must draw on knowledge or experience *external to the story*. There is indeed the potential for a larger myth operating within *In Country*—the quest, the journey in this case not for the burial but the honoring of the dead, and for the questioning of why they died—but the minimalist reader, immersed in the world of mass culture that Mason depicts so convincingly, staying within the filtering consciousness of Mason's point-of-view character, runs the danger of not realizing the power of that myth.

Thus one wonders, finally, if *In Country*, despite its many virtues, immerses itself too completely and uncritically in throwaway culture, and in the process—by showing us the world through the eyes of a character who focuses altogether on television and rock music and shopping malls—runs the risk of itself becoming a product of the throwaway culture it depicts, as lasting as and no more lasting than (that is, as dispensable as) *M*A*S*H* and rock music circa 1984. Perhaps not. *In Country*, despite its topicality, indeed transcends its decade in many ways. And perhaps we should not be troubled by a narrator whose idea of history goes back no further than the Beatles. Perhaps mythology—and a way to order one's life—can come from *M*A*S*H* as well as *The Golden Bough*. These are questions that Bobbie Ann Mason raises, questions of culture, and they are important ones for, among other things, southern literature. As recently as the 1920s and 1930s in many circles—and I think of H. L. Mencken's evaluations of the South or, in 1941, W. J. Cash's estimate—southern *culture* was judged deficient because, when they wrote, the South had little in the way of *high* culture: libraries, museums, theater, and so forth.[6] But the South had folk culture in abundance, black and white, and that culture is well recognized today. Mass culture—popular commercial culture—having fewer organic roots is harder to accept, its integrity harder to locate, but a writer such as Mason makes us encounter and consider it.

She makes us consider another matter as well, and one not often discussed: the importance and role of class in contemporary southern fiction. For one might contend that class—now that race and gender are being addressed—will be the next enlivening issue in the consideration of southern letters. Writers such as Bobbie Ann Mason and Jayne Anne Phillips are important in this regard. First, their very *names*—which are, after all, very average names, not quite proper in the way *Jimmy* Carter was not quite proper—must shock those who have been given reason to believe that a writer's name should be elegant and distinguished. Might one say, indeed, that what is happening in contemporary southern letters is, among other things, that same revolution in naming that took place in American literature a century and a quarter ago when those august triple-named demigods—Henry Wadsworth Longfellow, William Cullen Bryant, James Russell Lowell, John Greenleaf Whittier, and Ralph Waldo Emerson—gave way to plain "Walt Whitman" and (not even a true name) "Mark Twain."

But it is not naming but writing that concerns me here, and

not do only Mason and Phillips treat almost exclusively working class characters, but numerous other novelists—one thinks of Harry Crews and Richard Ford among others—write largely about them too. This, in itself, is not new. Southerners as far back as William Byrd and, a century later, the Southwest Humorists wrote about plain and poor whites, albeit with humor and condescension, and earlier in this century Faulkner, Erskine Caldwell, and Flannery O'Connor continued the treatment of humble whites. But what is new, or nearly so, is that Mason, Phillips, and Ford write about rural and urban working-class people unselfconsciously and, more to the point, approvingly. And what we see is more than that. Certainly Faulkner, too, approved of his plain white characters: V. K. Ratliff, the sewing-machine salesman in *The Hamlet,* and Byron Bunch in *Light in August* are among the most admirable characters in his fiction, and he never forgot that plain white Southerners usually had a dignity, an ethical sense, that distinguished them from the worst of the ethically poor white Snopeses. Faulkner *approved* of Ratliff and Byron Bunch, but that is not to say he identified with them. He linked himself, rather, with the Sartorises and the Compsons. Caldwell, O'Connor, and T. S. Stribling as well, not to mention Byrd and the earlier humorists, detached themselves from their plain whites. The idea that the imaginative writer was always a product of a "good family" had broken down in the rest of the United States about the time of Dreiser, but the assumption in the South, through the Renascence, was that the man and particularly the woman of letters, with few exceptions, came either from the gentry or from that educated class of public servants, teachers, and ministers—and the assumption was also the reality in most cases. In some of those few cases where origins were indeed humble, such as Katherine Anne Porter's, a privileged background was invented; in other cases where there was indeed some justification for claims of family prominence or privilege, the claim was often exaggerated.

One thinks of Faulkner (whose grandfather, after all, headed up support in Oxford for J. K. Vardaman, the race-baiting champion of Mississippi poor whites) who probably thought even more highly of the earlier Falkners than they deserved; and Allen Tate, who said that he didn't learn until he was thirty that he had been born in Kentucky, since his mother had always told him he was a Virginian.[7]

So class always mattered in the world of southern letters, although it was often obscured by race. But what is different now is that numerous younger southern writers—Mason and Ford, not to mention somewhat older writers such as Harry Crews and David Madden—do not come from the privileged classes, from educated families; and, unlike Katherine Anne Porter, they do not in any way try to disguise their origins. Mason comes from plain farming people in Kentucky, Crews from tenant farmers in Florida, Ford from working and lower-level business people, often on the move, in Arkansas and Mississippi. In their backgrounds there was very little in the way of family eminence, pretension, elevated pride, or—in Ford's case—even a sense of place or community or religious commitment. What I am coming to is that some of those qualities of southern writing and southern life identified and celebrated by the Southern Agrarians—who were by and large from landed or educated families, and usually both—were not representative of *all* Southerners. I mean qualities such as an awareness of history, a regard for tradition and hierarchy, an ornamental sense, even in certain respects a sense of place. And one of the reasons—only one—some southern fiction today does not seem to reflect these qualities is that it is written by *different* Southerners, not only black Southerners (who *do*, curiously, often embrace these qualities) but white Southerners whose families had little past to hold on to, little history in which ancestors had played important parts, little reason to live dramatically, little high culture to protect. Thus Mason in a *New York Times Maga-*

zine interview unapologetically defends, indeed embraces, popular culture. She finds no fault with people who spend their lives in front of the television set and walking through malls; and as for her, "Writing is my version of rock & roll." William Alexander Percy might look at K-Mart Realism and say that contemporary southern literature has followed the course of southern politics he decried in *Lanterns on the Levee:* that now the "bottom rail [is] on top."[8] But if one subscribes to an evolutionary theory of literature, which numbered William Dean Howells among its proponents in the late nineteenth century, what is happening is simply an expansion of the franchise, part of the centuries-old progress in Western literature from a writing by and principally about the privileged—though occasionally *about* the lower classes, comically rendered—to a literature by, and treating seriously, the common people.

2

I want to turn from class to apparent classlessness, from Mason's western Kentucky—which, despite her own unpretentiousness, spawned Mark Twain's proud aristocrats, the Grangerfords and Shepherdsons—to Lee Smith's southern Appalachia, classless that is (as Faulkner's Thomas Sutpen discovered) compared to the remainder of the South. Smith is a talented and prolific novelist: in her mid-forties, she has produced some eight novels and collections of stories. Most take place in her native southwest Virginia, and most are set in a world of contemporary popular culture, although that culture is usually in conflict with an older, organic Appalachian folk culture.[9] It is one of these novels, *Oral History,* the work I believe to be her finest, that I should like to consider.

The novel, Smith's fifth, is an ambitious undertaking, partly family chronicle, partly folklore and cultural anthropology, part elegy and part satire. It brings together in stark contrast the old world of mountain clannishness, superstition, blood feuds, dulcimers, quilts, and Appalachian speech and that invading world of mass commercial culture. One sees that contrast from the beginning as city-bred Jennifer, the college-student granddaughter of the mountain Cantrells, comes to Hoot Owl Holler for the first time both to complete an oral history project and to find her roots. The story begins with Little Luther, whom Jennifer believes to be her grandfather, sitting on the porch of the new house playing his dulcimer and singing "in a high bluegrass falsetto" while his wife, Ora Mae, "as big and shapeless as a rock," sits outside in a chair brought down from the old house, now said to be haunted, in Hoot Owl Holler—a chair that can't go in the new house because it doesn't go with her daughter-in-law's "living-room suite, which is Mediterranean." In motion around Luther and Ora Mae are their son Almarine, an AmWay employee who is busy putting down orange shag carpet inside; his wife, Debra, who is wearing pink knit slacks and "a black T-shirt with 'Foxy Lady' written on it in silver glitter"; and their two sons, who are running into the house to see "Magnum" on television.[10]

Meanwhile Jennifer, having left her tape recorder in the empty old house on the hill in order to pick up any sounds of ghosts, records in a notebook impressions of her relatives and their world. "The salt of the earth," she writes (p. 4). "The picturesque old homeplace sits so high on the hill that it leaves one with the aftertaste of judgment in his or her mouth. Looking out from its porch, one sees the panorama of the whole valley spread out like a picture" (p. 6). She has come to the mountains of Virginia, she writes, to "expand my consciousness, my tolerance, my depth" (p. 8), and she has found it "just beautiful . . . and these . . . people so sweet, so simple, so kind. . . . And Little Luther, what a character" (p. 4). She ends her notebook entry—"I shall descend now, to be with them as they go about their evening chores" (p. 8) —and when she reaches the new house she says to Ora Mae, who she believes is her grandmother: "I think it's just wonderful the way all of you live right here in this valley and help each other out" (p. 10). "Extended family situation," she thinks, but it is too dark to write in the notebook so she sits back and listens to Little Luther playing "Fox on the Run," hears the boys turning up the television so they can hear over Luther's music, and wishes all of a sudden she were back at college or "back in her father's house watching Masterpiece Theater" (p. 11).

This is all a little heavy-handed, of course, as obvious a critique of social science, over-intellectualizing, and abstraction on Smith's part as, say, Flannery O'Connor's portrait of the schoolteacher, Rayber, who with his papers and charts "studies" old Tarwater in *The Violent Bear It Away*. Jennifer's language alone convicts her. The word "picturesque" implies detachment, seeing something from the point of view of another culture, having it conform to a particular image in her mind. The valley, "spread out like a picture," is seen equally abstractly—a picture she has seen before (not precisely this picture but this *kind* of picture), one that is more real to her than what she is in fact now seeing. One thinks of Walker Percy's remark in *The Message in the Bottle* about those who, seeing the Grand Canyon for the first time, feel they have seen it before; they *have*, in a picture that looks even more spectacular than what they are now seeing.[11] Jennifer sees the valley with the eyes of one who has had a course in Appalachian life, approaching mountain culture historically, anthropologically, sociologically—but not giving herself to it, becoming part of it.

Jennifer's closing notebook entry "I shall descend now . . ." suggests an even greater detachment, a complete division between seer and what is seen, an intense self-consciousness. And we have further evidence of her detachment in her wish that she were home *looking* at something else, *Masterpiece Theater*. That is the final variety of culture Smith packs into her opening pages.

After the folk culture of Little Luther and Ora Mae and the mass culture of television and silver glitter, we have the high culture —or what would be seen in America as high culture—of Alistair Cooke and *Masterpiece Theater.* Folk culture, the most indigenous, should be the most natural, the least self-conscious of the three, but one realizes at the outset that in a world in which folklorists and oral historians come calling, even that is in danger of becoming acutely stylized and self-conscious. Indeed, Little Luther already knows he is something of—as Jennifer calls him —a character. Curiously, in this holler in the Appalachians, it is mass culture—"Magnum," Charlie's Angels dolls, and "Foxy Lady"—which is least self-conscious of all. In any case, we realize after the opening pages that this is very much a novel *about* culture. Each of the three varieties competes with the others, just as the sounds of "Magnum" compete with those of Little Luther's dulcimer, and Smith leaves us to ponder the relationship among the three.

Jennifer, as I have suggested, is hardly new in southern literature. Not only does she resemble, in her desire to "study" a culture, O'Connor's Rayber, but also, in a somewhat different manner—a more favorable, more serious portrait—James Agee's description of himself in *Let Us Now Praise Famous Men,* another work in which a citified, over-educated Southerner, long removed from his humble roots, returns to spend time with people (not literally *his* relatives) who live as he imagines one side of his own family had lived. It is, of course, not quite the same thing: Agee never completely broke through the abstraction or shed the self-consciousness either, but at least he was acutely aware of the effort that had to be made. If—through eating the greasy food of his sharecropper hosts and sleeping in their bug-infested beds and, more important, taking them on their own terms—he could not altogether will himself into their community, he made an effort far more valiant than Jennifer's. Her failure is not her fault, of course, any more than Sam's incomplete historical understanding in *In Country* is her fault, since Jennifer, as fully as Sam, has been conditioned in a particular manner—in her case, to see these mountaineers as simple and quaint—and has been assigned by her oral history professor the task of "interpreting" them. One at first might contend that Lee Smith, although she takes pains to distance herself from Jennifer, is not really so far removed from her character. She herself, to a certain extent, is doing what Jennifer does: serving us up amateur folklore and anthropology, even if with the intent of satirizing that very practice. Smith is not Jennifer, however, because her larger vision is not at all abstract, not sociological. Aside from the opening scene—which *is* rather contrived, which tells more than shows—Smith is concerned with individual lives, individual stories, with dramatizing rather than interpreting.

From that point on, *Oral History* is an interconnecting series of stories about members of the Cantrell family and their neighbors around Hoot Owl Holler, stories which in the process of their unfolding reveal to the reader the truth about Jennifer's "roots," although that is hardly their primary function. Two of the principal narrators in this "oral history"—stories which are not told to Jennifer at all (she disappears for most of the novel) but rather to us or, by suggestion, to the author—are Granny Younger and Rose Hibbitts, two women who were around before the turn of the century. The stories they tell are of the original Almarine Cantrell, his witch woman Red Emmy, his beloved wife Pricey Jane, and his mysterious second wife, Vashti. But as her narrators tell their stories, it becomes clear that Smith's novel is really, in part, about the reliability of oral history itself. Oral history, of course, has gained a fine reputation in recent years for being "the real story," authentic history about authentic people, as opposed to "official" accounts of history, often supporting an "official" position, concerning wars, elections, legislation, and people in the mass. What we find here however, as we listen to Granny, Rose Hibbitts, and other tellers—and to Richard Burlage, the outsider from Richmond who writes rather than speaks his story—is that these stories are sometimes at variance with each other, are no more authentic or reliable, no more "truthful," than official and conventional varieties of history. Both Granny and, particularly, Rose have personal stakes in the stories they tell, both emphasize certain facts in order to arrive at certain versions of the truth. What we learn, finally, is that what we have thought to be "true," what Jennifer to the last assumes to be true, is in fact not true: Ora Mae and Little Luther are not her grandparents after all; rather Burlage—who isn't even aware that he has children in Appalachia, much less grandchildren—and Ora Mae's sister Dory are her grandparents. Nor does Jennifer ever learn the truth about her mother's death: she does not know that her mother became sexually involved with a high school boy, became pregnant (either by the boy or by her cousin Billy), and died of complications of pregnancy. Rather, Jennifer believes her mother died of pneumonia.

As in Faulkner's *Absalom, Absalom!*, the reader finally knows more of the truth than any of the individual narrators, but the deeper truth of both novels is that truth itself is not only a relative but a highly elusive thing. So is Appalachian culture, like any indigenous culture that does not yield up its secrets easily. Although Smith does not explore such possibilities, *mining* could be seen as the operative metaphor of the novel. Just as outside interests have dug into the hills of Appalachia for coal and other mineral wealth, now folklorists and oral historians mine the hills for stories, legends, and what they hope will be Elizabethan English. The deeper "truth" of *Oral History* is that one cannot, with notebook, tape recorder, and camera, *capture* the mountains—any more than the ice cutters in Thoreau's *Walden* (whose ice began to melt when it left its point of origin) could capture the pond.

It is the individual stories then, and not any attempt to abstract the mind and temper of the hill people, that gives *Oral History* its power, and we see in their stories what Jennifer never sees: that the "mountain people" are like other people, no more and no less "sweet" or "simple." Smith resists the temptation to summarize or interpret until the end—when, as in the beginning of the novel, the hand of the author lies heavy. There is also a lot of sheer funning in Smith's conclusion, as in her beginning, almost a parody of the usual conclusion to an ambitious family chronicle:

> Eventually, Debra will have a hysterectomy. Roscoe will win a Morehead Scholarship to the University of North Carolina; Troy will start a rock group; Sally and Roy will buy a retirement house at Claytor Lake where they will continue to live out their long and happy lives; Suzy Q will marry young; old Richard Burlage will write his memoirs and they will be published, to universal if somewhat limited acclaim, by LSU Press; . . . Al will be elected president of the Junior Toastmasters Club. Then he will make a killing in AmWay and retire from it young, sinking his money in land. He will be a major investor in the ski run which will be built, eventually, on the side of Black Rock Mountain. The success of this enterprise will inspire him to embark on his grandest plan yet: Ghostland, the wildly successful theme park and recreation area (campground, motel, Olympic-size pool, waterslide and gift shop) in Hoot Owl Holler. Ghostland, designed by a Nashville architect, will be the prettiest theme park east of Opryland itself, its rides and amusements terraced up and down the steep holler, its skylift zooming up and down from the burial ground where the cafeteria is. And the old homeplace still stands, smack in the middle of Ghostland, untouched. Vines grow up through the porch

> where the rocking chair sits, and the south wall of the house has fallen in. It's surrounded by a chain link fence, fronted by the observation deck with redwood benches which fill up every summer night at sunset with those who have paid the extra $4.50 to be here, to sit in this cool misty hush while the shadows lengthen from the three mountains—Hoot Owl, Snowman, and Hurricane—while the night settles in, to be here when dark comes and the wind and the laughter start, to see it with their own eyes when that rocking chair starts rocking and rocks like crazy the whole night long. [p. 292]

Smith saves herself at least a hundred pages in thus concluding, and if in her summation she violates Henry James's dictum —*dramatize*, not tell—she does reflect rather accurately what is happening in the Sun Belt South, even in its upper reaches. What we have at the end of *Oral History* is a blending of cultures in the worst possible manner: the indigenous folk culture turns into a cheap imitation of itself for the sake of commercial mass culture. What once was organic and natural becomes cheap and tawdry (if sanitized), what once was authentic and distinctive becomes stylized. Jennifer's vision is validated after all: everyone *will* see the mountain people as sweet, mountain culture as quaint.

High culture, of course, is neglected in the conclusion. It plays little part in the book, in fact, save in Jennifer's early reference to *Masterpiece Theater* and, in a more significant way, in the person of Richard Burlage of Richmond. For, in one respect, this is a novel not only about Appalachian culture but a commentary on an older southern subject—the meaning of Virginia —and Burlage is a representative of that more celebrated Virginia culture: genteel, Episcopalian James River civilization, sophisticated and even, to some extent, intellectually engaged. Burlage is a product of William Byrd's Virginia, and the mountaineers representatives of the hinterland, the Virginia frontier which Byrd found crude and barbaric, exceeded in its benightedness only by North Carolina. Burlage comes from that Virginia of hierarchy and class consciousness, the Virginia that opened Thomas Sutpen's eyes after Sutpen, with his father, came out of the classless society of the western Virginia hills. The world of Burlage's origins has often been portrayed as the *best* of Virginia, the best of the South, that ideal that Sutpen carried with him into the new Cotton Kingdom.

But such is not the case in *Oral History*. Here all is reversed. The well-born Burlage, a curious combination of cavalier and puritan, comes to the hills in search of "naturalness," a "simpler era," but it is he, not the mountaineers, who is made to look foolish, insensitive, self-indulgent. His problem—fully as much as Thomas Sutpen's, although in a profoundly different way—is innocence, an innocence of the ways of the hills just as profound as Sutpen's of the Tidewater, an inability to recognize that "mountain people" are, first and foremost, *people*, not rustics. Burlage is overly civilized, lacking vitality and substance, is the kind of modernist, self-conscious, abstracted, well-bred southern male who also populates the fiction of Percy, the poetry and fiction (*The Fathers*) of Tate. The heir of a class that preached and sometimes even practiced *noblesse oblige*, he leaves behind the young mountain woman who will bear his twins. He does not know she is pregnant, but neither does he try very hard to find out. He sends one note to her—it goes astray—and makes no other effort to reach the woman he says he has loved beyond imagining.

The most serious indictment in *Oral History* (more serious than that of popular culture), then, is drawn against Burlage and the civilization he represents. Folk society is hardly idealized in the novel: it contains neither the strong sense of community nor the religious sense one idealizes, and the proof of its relative weakness is that it falls so easily before popular culture in the end. But whatever its weaknesses, folk culture fares much better than the civilized Virginia to which Burlage is heir. It is not Smith's primary intention to make such a statement—none of her characters is particularly aware of class and she is anything but a didactic writer—but such is the impression that emerges. For a novel about a classless society is finally, despite itself, very much a statement about class.

3

That leaves one writer—perhaps the boldest, zaniest, and most outrageous writer of the contemporary South—whose work I also want to discuss in the light of traditional southern culture and the new Sun Belt dispensation. Barry Hannah's world is far from Smith's Appalachia and Mason's western Kentucky. It is the Deep South, what Virginians in the nineteenth century called the Far South, that is, Hannah's native Mississippi as well as its bordering states Alabama and Louisiana—that area long assumed to be the most benighted part of the benighted South, the truest home of southern racial conflict, religious frenzy, and general cultural deprivation. Hannah's fiction includes some of that, particularly in his first novel *Geronimo Rex* (1972), but mainly the world he presents is a world of Deep South suburbs, country clubs, and small university towns—a world, however, that is no less bizarre for all its trappings of civilization. In the 1980s Hannah was the chronicler of the craziest edges of that world. After his novel *Ray* appeared in 1980, he was touted as nothing less than a phenomenon in American fiction, the literary drug of choice for avant garde readers—"the best fiction writer to appear in the South since Flannery O'Connor," according to Larry McMurtry; a writer for whom the critic requires "a fresh lingo to do justice to [the] magic, mystery, and hilarity," according to Benjamin DeMott.[12]

DeMott said in the same review that Hannah is as close as one can come in contemporary fiction to being a writer free from literary influence, a writer without precedent, but there he is surely wrong. For Hannah is at one and the same time the nearest thing to a postmodernist among under-fifty southern novelists *and* a writer more concerned with the southern literary past than nearly any other southern writer of his time. He is an heir to several southern literary traditions, not the least of which are Southwest Humor and Southern Gothic. Hannah is, in his way, nothing less than a teller of tall tales, retaining the exaggeration and the raucousness, even inhabiting the exact geographical precincts (Mississippi and Alabama) of the Old Southwest. What else is his portrait in *The Tennis Handsome* of the corpse of Dr. Jimmy Word floating down the Mississippi from Vicksburg to New Orleans:

> so dried out and light-boned, he floated on his back . . . bobbing in the drift, turning slowly around. But some leftover mad alligator below Natchez got to him. When he floated by Baton Rouge, he looked like a harmonica—his ribs, etc. Some casual darkie, alone on the levee, playing his tonette, may have seen a weird roil in the Big Muddy, a rolling of bones and cloth shreds.
>
> Word slept with the fish. Like them he made friends with the continental sewage of the Mississippi. . . . Then the rain came so hard, it stood up his corpse and the corpse began walking, sometimes almost water-skiing when a gust hit it just right.[13]

Such a passage is reminiscent not only of the overstatement of the Old Southwest but also of the grotesquerie of a more recent literary tradition, Southern Gothic. Indeed, Hannah is (as I have noted) one of the leading practitioners of a sort of neo–Southern Gothic, a depicter not only of corpses bobbing down the Mississippi but of living creatures, haunted, violent, both frightened and frightening. And he is, as well, an heir to the southern literary tradition in his very love of language, his *confidence* with language, his cadences, his voice—particularly in *Geronimo Rex* (if not the later books) subscribing to that wisdom accepted by most southern writers, both nineteenth century and twentieth, both good and bad, both Thomas Nelson Page and William Faulkner, that nothing should be said in ten words that cannot be said more elegantly in twenty.

It is Faulkner and Thomas Wolfe, among others, who would seem to be Hannah's ancestors, although Faulkner in ways that go beyond literary influence. It is the figure Hannah has cultivated that in certain respects recalls Faulkner—a Mississippian of small stature but large ambition, with a love of airplanes, alcohol, and other traditional southern male pursuits, possessing an abundance of confidence to undertake the unusual, and given to a certain mythmaking about himself. Hannah's first novel, *Geronimo Rex*, published when he was twenty-nine, won the William Faulkner Prize; at forty he moved to Oxford and has lived since then in William Faulkner's hometown.

But as for strictly literary influence—aside from a love of language, an attraction to the grotesque, and a penchant for the *tour de force*—Hannah does not seem to be a direct descendant of Faulkner. Lacking the tragic sense, devoid of Faulkner's high seriousness and social consciousness, he is not the *moralist* that Faulkner, in the broadest sense of that term, often is. Hannah himself has said that Hemingway influenced him more than Faulkner did, and in several ways—in the highly autobiographical nature of his fiction, the sheer gusto, and the rebelliousness of his early work manifesting itself in a revolt from the village—it would appear that Thomas Wolfe influenced him more than either. Hannah has spoken of his admiration for Wolfe, both for *Look Homeward, Angel* and for Wolfe's conception of himself as an artist: "There's a kind of ambitious grandness to Wolfe and

Henry Miller and Faulkner that the contemporary mind simply does not want to face."[14] *Geronimo Rex*, a lengthy *bildungsroman*, is about Harry Monroe, a budding writer who, like Eugene Gant, wants nothing more than to flee from the Old South (although, like Eugene, he is still drawn to that earlier South). Harry is, in many respects, Hannah himself, resembling his creator in looks (the facial features of an American Indian), musical interests, and education in a small Mississippi Baptist college and, later, in the University of Arkansas English department. The autobiographical impulse is even more noticeable in *Ray*, a novel set in Tuscaloosa, where Hannah lived and taught for five years, a work in which Hannah's children and several of his University of Alabama colleagues appear by name and in which the protagonist's father, like Hannah's father, is said to have roomed at Ole Miss with Senator James Eastland. And one finds, not surprisingly, that the names of both protagonists—Harry and Ray—are derived from the name Barry Hannah.

Geronimo Rex is a far more traditional novel than *Ray*, or anything else Hannah has written since. It is concerned with—if in an iconoclastic manner—family, religion, place, history, all the old concerns of his predecessors. One finds racial tension and violence, a healthy dose of the grotesque (in Lepoyster, the racial fanatic, as well as in some of Harry's girlfriends), and a trip to Vicksburg in search of a historical and family past. Harry sees the battlefield and the monuments—"I pitied the idiots who cared for such scenes. I was among the idiots who cared for such scenes"—looks from the bluff down into the town of Vicksburg and sees the house in which his mother ("the most-adored piece either side of the river") had grown up, and listens to his friend Fleece explain "about when cotton was king in 1850." All the while he observes "the struggling remains of riverside Pharaohism—the restaurants advertising fresh river catfish, the plasticolored motels, the antique shops, the bait and snack stores." It is all terribly sad to Harry: "Vicksburg simply weighed on my heart like lumber: all the old history, all the ravaged guntoters, all of contemporary Vicksburg; Grandmother's house, how it seemed like a boat rotting up in a bayou nobody would ever find."[15]

If *Geronimo Rex* is a well-made novel, nearly of the old school, Hannah's novels of the eighties, *Ray, The Tennis Handsome,* and *Hey Jack!*, are his signature works, the books reviewers have in mind when they call him something new in southern fiction. In these novels Hannah is still ambitious, although ambition is no longer to be measured by the number of words between covers. *Ray* is barely a hundred pages long, *The Tennis Handsome* and *Hey Jack!* not a great deal longer. *Ray,* Hannah's version of fear and loathing in Tuscaloosa, is narrated by Dr. Ray, an alcoholic physician unable to heal himself. An ex-pilot who flew, or claims to have flown, support missions for B-52 bombers in Vietnam, he speaks at first from a hospital where he is patient, not doctor, and what we hear are his adventures and misadventures with a cast of zany characters in Alabama. In one respect, Hannah belongs to the guns-guts-and-glory world of southern thought: he is, among other things, a very *offensive* writer, or at least one whose characters talk casually about gooks, queers, and niggers and have yet to have their collective consciousness raised in regard to women. In another respect, it might be claimed, Hannah writes a critique of that southern world. In either case this is not a world overflowing with sweet reasonableness. Neither is it exactly the older benighted South. Rather, it is a world of Lear jets, fast cars, easy sex and drugs, high-tech rockabilly, new-style misogyny, and general social and cultural fragmentation—a postmodern South in which place, community, traditional family, and even class play little part. Nor does religion: the role of the Baptist minister of Ray's acquaintance is to dispense not forgiveness but Valium, and finally to commit murder. And, for once, the southern writer inhabiting the postmodern world is close to being a postmodern writer himself. Form reflects substance, both chaotic, and this is almost but not quite the self-conscious art of John Barth, a story about the telling of the story, a work in which—because of the mental condition of the narrator and thus the way in which he tells the story—truth, reliability, and fiction itself are called into question. The narrative voice is slick, hip—and desperate. Ray speaks of himself in the third person part of the time, uncertain where he is going with his story, and near the end he loses control altogether, units of thought becoming increasingly briefer, more and more fragmented.

One of the things that confuse Ray, but also obsess him, is history, an unlikely preoccupation for a man so situated in the ahistorical postmodern world. But Ray could never say, with Mason's Emmett, "We can't learn from history"; to the contrary, if anything, he has learned too much, finds too overwhelming the power of the past in the present. Hannah is able to do in *Ray*, through the sick and overloaded mind of his protagonist, what Mason, through the sound but understimulated mind of hers, is unable to do—recognize, *feel*, the relationship between Vietnam and the American Civil War, indeed recognize the relationships among all wars. Ray's thoughts of his experience in Southeast Asia turn into visions of fighting in the Maryland hills with Jeb Stuart, wiping out all the Federals but one:

> We threw earth over the dead. Stuart went out in the forest and wept.
>
> *Then all of us slept. Too many dead.*
> *Let us hie to Virginia, let us flee.*
>
> I fell asleep with the banjo music in my head and I dreamed of two whores sucking me. . . .
>
> I live in so many centuries. Everybody is still alive. [p. 41]

Ray is Hannah's Gerontion—or, better, the Tiresias of Eliot's *The Waste Land*—unable to forget. Nightmares both of Vietnam and the Civil War come with increasing frequency: "Oh, help me! I am losing myself in two centuries and two wars" (p. 45). Finally, visions of Civil War and Vietnam merge, Ray confusing the two, not knowing which he is fighting. Sabers and phantom jets are one.

They *are* one, Hannah suggests, just as past and present are highly relative. It is a conclusion reached not only by Ray but by his friend Charlie DeSoto, manager of the soap factory south of town and descendant, he believes, of Hernando de Soto. Charlie loses himself in accounts of the original de Soto's expedition from Florida to what is now Alabama, as related in the diary of de Soto's companion Rangel. Charlie is especially attentive to a passage about the reported slaughter of four thousand Indians, including Chief Tuskaloosa, since the passage reminds him "of the adventurous perversity in himself that he cherished" (p. 15). Charlie DeSoto recognizes the difference between past and present more clearly than Ray, but he too is one of unsettled mind, sometimes overcome by rage toward those he sees at random: "It is terribly, excruciatingly difficult to be at peace, thought DeSoto, when all our history is war" (p. 16).

What sort of commentary on history is this? Is it not better, after all, to live in Mason's world of the near-eternal present if a knowledge of the past leads, as in Ray's and Charlie's cases, to an unhealthful obsession with the past, in Ray's case to an inability to distinguish past from present? The answer, of course, is that over-indulgence in anything leads to an unbalanced life, although it also leads to a rich and full fiction. A knowledge of the past is especially painful when one realizes, as Hannah's characters do, that things never were as good as an unexamined past would have them, and that they probably never will be. Ray's contemplation of the Civil War, as Charlie's of de Soto, reinforces no heroic vision; but it is closer to the truth than the traditional idea of war, the Civil War in particular, in the southern imagination. What Ray and Charlie find is that, after all, the past mirrors the present, or vice versa. The grotesque and the pathos of present-day Tuscaloosa—the "evil" of the preacher Maynard Castro, the love-starved clerks, the man who can't talk because a cottonmouth bit him on the tongue when he was a child—all find their parallels in the past.

There is little redemption, then, anywhere in *Ray*, nor in Hannah's later, even more bizarre work, *The Tennis Handsome* (1983). This novel, too, is set in the prosperous postguilt Newest of New Souths—an even more affluent part of it, largely Louisiana just before the mid-eighties Oil Bust—and it is even more violent, more given to Sun Belt Gothic than its predecessor. The story is too involved to summarize easily, but one gets some idea of what Hannah is about by reviewing his cast of leading characters: French Edward, a brain-damaged tennis handsome who dedicates his victories to, among other things, Save-the-Whales; James Word, a bisexual botany professor whom we met earlier floating down the Mississippi (into which he had fallen in an embrace with French Edward); Dr. Baby Levaster, Edward's sometimes-keeper who runs a street clinic in New Orleans; and Bobby Smith, another of Hannah's haunted, homophobic Vietnam vets.

This novel, unlike *Ray*, makes no pretense of being a meditation on history—other than Vietnam, in Smith's case, and painful personal histories here and there (although, even in this novel as in several other Hannah stories, Jeb Stuart creeps in). Here the present is most important, and Hannah's dazzling prose and outrageous comic vision make the present seem almost sufficient, aesthetically at least. This is the South, to a great extent, toward which Hannah's work has been moving, the Sun Belt South in which, artistically, he is most at home. It is a world more than a little familiar to anyone acquainted with southern fiction of the past quarter-century: an affluent, newly confident Louisiana, Mississippi, and Alabama of country clubs and glassy houses with backyard pools and overhanging pines; of doctors, dentists, and other well-heeled professional men who play golf and tennis, and cool, elegant, and sometimes devious women who spend their time doing watercolors; people searching for identity and trying infidelity. Both *The Tennis Handsome* and *Ray*—with its satire, its cool understanding of the contemporary South, its narrator telling his story from a mental hospital, even its good fun at the expense of "silly" Ohio—are reminiscent of another southern voice. Barry Hannah throws in a few more crazies, is a little more lewd, outrageous, and grotesque, less thoughtful, philosophical, and spiritual, but in most other respects this is the world of Walker Percy's fiction. Percy got there first, but, as we shall subsequently see, Hannah isn't the only southern writer who has staked a late claim to it.

3

Richard Ford and Josephine Humphreys: Walker Percy in New Jersey and Charleston

Richard Ford and Josephine Humphreys, both writers in their mid-forties, came of age in the lower South at a time just before and during the civil rights movement and, after that time, found themselves suddenly in a position unknown since the 1830s, southern writers in an unfallen world. The case of Humphreys as a southern writer is somewhat easier to deal with: a native of Charleston who attended Duke University, she returned to Charleston to live and write. Ford's case is more complicated, and I should like to consider that first.

Richard Ford is a most uncommon southern writer. On the surface, his southern credentials are convincing enough: he was born in 1944 in Jackson, Mississippi, and grew up in Jackson, ten miles away from and two years younger than Barry Hannah in Clinton. As a child he lived next door to the Jefferson Davis School and across the street from the house where Eudora Welty had lived as a child thirty-five years before. But Ford left the South at eighteen and lived elsewhere for nearly a quarter-century, and only one of his works—he has written three novels and a volume of stories—has been set in the South. That novel, *A Piece of My Heart* (1974), takes place largely on an island in the Mississippi

River between Mississippi and Arkansas, and in it are touches of Faulkner and also perhaps Cormac McCarthy. Each of the next three works is set in a different part of North America, *The Ultimate Good Luck* (1981) in Mexico, *The Sportswriter* (1986) in the Northeast and upper Midwest, and the highly praised collection of stories, *Rock Springs* (1987), largely in Montana. And for reasons other than location, Ford's best and best-known work, *The Sportswriter*, seems to have very little in common with the traditional southern novel.

Nor does Ford, in his choice of residence or his remarks on writing, demonstrate any particular allegiance to geographical place, southern or otherwise. Bruce Weber, writing in the *New York Times Magazine*, has called him "possibl[y] America's most peripatetic fiction writer," and Ford, who lived in Michigan, New Jersey, Mexico, and Montana, among other places, before returning to "the sticks of Mississippi" (as he puts it), and who now lives in New Orleans, acknowledges that he finds it hard to stay put residentially or artistically. "I try to exhaust my own interest in a place," he has said. "Then I'll just move on, write about someplace else where I kind of notice again how people accommodate themselves to where they live." Place he defines as "wherever we can find dominion over our subject and make it convincing."[1] It is nearly a postmodern definition of place.

If, then, a devotion to place—generally, a particular place—defines the southern writer, one would have to conclude that Ford is no southern writer at all. But he is, very much so, as I hope to demonstrate, and again it seems to me, as I suggested in the discussion of Bobbie Ann Mason, that the problem lies with a particular definition of the southern literary imagination, which has been, in some respects, too narrow. It is doubtless true that *most* southern writers, for reasons growing out of the regional location and experience, have been more devoted to place and to history than most nonsouthern ones—but not all southern writers.

"We were not a family," Ford has said, "for whom history had much to offer,"[2] and he could have said the same thing for place. Ford knew that his mother had been born in a dirt-floor cabin in Arkansas—and that there was Indian blood in his maternal grandmother's family—but he had no idea of his mother's *father's* birthplace or national origin. Ford's father was a country boy who quit school in the seventh grade, worked for a time as a produce stocker for a grocery store, and later became a starch salesman, traveling through the Deep South. Ford's parents lived partly on the road in the early years of their marriage, and moved to Jackson only shortly before their only child was born. The young Richard Ford traveled with his father on sales trips through Mississippi, Arkansas, and Louisiana; he also, in his early teens, had a few minor scrapes with the law. Ford's father died when he was sixteen, and two years after that, after spending summers with his grandfather, who managed a hotel in Little Rock, Ford went off to Michigan State University to study hotel administration.

Such is hardly the biography of a Southern Agrarian. Ford belongs, as does Mason, quite literally to a different *class* of writers. He did not come to literature because of family tradition or interests—as a teenager he cared far more for cars and bird hunting than for books—but rather because, at Michigan State, he discovered Faulkner, particularly *Absalom, Absalom!* Reading in his room in East Lansing about Thomas Sutpen was hardly the same as that other transplanted Mississippian, Quentin, talking about Sutpen in his college rooms in Cambridge, but Sutpen's story and the way Faulkner told it fascinated him. It was reading Faulkner, Ford later said, as much as anything else that made him determine to become a writer.[3]

If at first (after brief attempts at law school and teaching) Ford attempted to write fiction like Faulkner's—as reviewers noted when *A Piece of My Heart* appeared—he also was looking to Hemingway, and that first novel, in fact, betrays more of

Hemingway's influence than Faulkner's. The setting on the Mississippi is reminiscent of Faulkner's "Old Man," and a sure touch with plain white Southerners, a certain mythic sense, a narrative complexity, and occasionally the style are Faulknerian. But the dominant style, the pace of the story, the tough-guy tone, and, between chapters, the short semi-autobiographical segments recalling childhood (as in *In Our Time*) resemble more nearly Hemingway. The story involves two men who come, for differing reasons, from distant locations—Robard Hewes from California for the love of a woman, Sam Newell from Chicago because he's falling apart—to the remote island in the Mississippi, and one of the men, Newell, is more than a little autobiographical: a native Mississippian, studying law in the North, whose father, a traveling starch salesman (the possibilities in that are endless for fiction) in Louisiana, Arkansas, and Mississippi, had suffered a heart attack and needed company on the road.

A Piece of My Heart is a violent book, and so are *The Ultimate Good Luck*—another Hemingway-like effort which deals with the Mexican drug trade—and *Rock Springs*, stories influenced by Hemingway, Sherwood Anderson, and possibly Ford's friend Raymond Carver. In these three works Ford seemed to have staked out his territory—backwoods country, unsentimental tone, and low-life characters, some running from the law, others running for other reasons. Those who called this minimalist fiction were, in the main, on target: Ford's characters live from day to day, having few goals save peace of mind, sex, freedom from the law, and enough money to get by. It was also a fiction in which Ford seemed to have put his southern origins behind him for good; except for a character or two who talk like Flannery O'Connor characters, there is almost nothing in this body of work to remind us that the author comes from the American South.

But Ford's ability to change places is matched only by his ability to change voices and literary modes, and his novel *The*

Sportswriter is as different from his other work as it is possible for a work by the same author to be. In this novel Ford leaves behind backwoods and low life for eastern suburbs and educated professionals, and no one could call *The Sportswriter* minimalist fiction. It is extravagant fiction, and also very wise. But no one called it southern fiction either, and seemingly for good reason. It takes place largely in New Jersey, partly in Michigan, and—for its last nine pages—in a very unsouthern part of southern Florida. *The Sportswriter* is a superb novel, a suggestive and richly allusive novel, but one which seems to have very little to do with Dixie. Ford might be a Southerner by birth, but if one searches for the postsouthern, post-Christian southern novel, this appears at first glance to be it.

Ford's narrator-protagonist Frank Bascombe had been born in the South, but that seems to have been largely an accident of geography. Now, thirty-eight and prosperous, he doesn't put much stock in those things that are supposed to concern Southerners —history, place, religion, family, community, race, or southern mythology. An ex-novelist and currently a writer for a slick sports magazine that sounds like *Sports Illustrated,* he has lived in suburban Haddam, New Jersey, within commuting distance of New York, since he sold movie rights to a novel some years before. He lives, it is clear, in John Cheever country, not William Faulkner or even Walker Percy country. His primary concerns as we meet him are coming to terms with the grief he has felt over the death of his nine-year-old son, Ralph, and the breakup of his marriage not long after his son's death. As the novel begins, after meeting his former wife at their son's grave Good Friday morning—which also happens to be Ralph's birthday—Frank takes off for Detroit to interview a paralyzed famous ex-football player. He is accompanied by his new girlfriend, Vicki Arcenault. He will return the next day, having had a disastrous interview and having concluded that things won't work out with Vicki. He will nonetheless have

Easter dinner with Vicki's family, learn of the suicide that afternoon of a fellow member of the Divorced Men's Club, and take the train later that night into New York to his magazine's midtown offices.

Frank, as I have said, has little regard for the past, and little apparent interest in it. "All we really want," he says early, "is to get to the point where the past can explain nothing about us and we can get on with life. Whose history can ever reveal very much? In my view Americans put too much emphasis on their pasts as a way of defining themselves, which can be death-dealing." And again, "I am a proponent of . . . forgetting. Forgetting dreams, grievances, old flaws in character—mine and others'. To me there is no hope unless we can forget what's said and gone before, and forgive it."[4]

Frank, then, loves to live in the present, in the material world, the consumer world, and Ford the novelist approaches that world as unapologetically as Frank (or as Bobbie Ann Mason), refusing to be judgmental, declining even to be ironic, at least in his remarks on that world (although not in other particulars). The question of irony, or lack of it, in dealing with mass culture in *The Sportswriter* is one that must be considered, one that goes to the heart of the novel. One would assume, as several reviewers did, that Ford *is* being ironic in dealing with the excesses of American commercial culture: how, one might ask, could a writer of Ford's keen eye and discrimination fail to be? But I am not so sure. Ford is indeed a discriminating writer, but he is also a writer who would object less to the excesses of popular culture than to a particular view—call it elitist or privileged—that would pass judgment on that culture. It is precisely this resistance to easy irony, a resisting the *temptation* to be ironic in dealing with popular culture, that distinguishes Ford from numerous other contemporary writers; for if an ironic vision is generally assumed to be a literary virtue, such a transcendence of accessible irony—or, perhaps, a deeper irony that turns on itself, ironizing the ironists—may be even more desirable. As concerns Frank Bascombe, Ford's hero is given to looking through mail-order catalogs: "I loved the idea of merchandise, and I loved those ordinary good American faces pictured there, people wearing their asbestos welding aprons, holding their cane fishing rods" (p. 196). He is indeed drawn to what others would call bad taste—the Arcenaults' house with its life-sized crucifix in Sherri-Lyn Woods, the Arcenaults' poodle named Elvis—and views it all with fascination, without a hint of condescension, and, again, almost without irony. Frank is a good man but not a religious one—in many ways, a spiritual man but not a religious one. He finds his answers to life's puzzles in a palmist. He is at home in the world of things, and he knows in part why he is drawn to things, to mail-order catalogs: "In me it fostered an odd assurance that some things outside my life were okay still" (p. 196).[5] And for the same reason he looks at Johnny Carson, or at the NBA Knicks and Cavaliers on television, *even* the Knicks and the Cavaliers, who were very bad in 1984. The game engages him, distracts him, keeps him from facing the abyss.

Frank Bascombe is a man who assures us not only that the past means nothing to him, but that family, at least ancestral family, counts for nothing. "Does it seem strange that I do not have a long and storied family history?" he asks. "Or a list of problems and hatreds to brood about—a bill of particular grievances and nostalgias that pretend to explain or trouble everything?" (p. 29). "The stamp of our parents on us and of the past in general is, to my mind, overworked, since at some point we are whole and by ourselves upon the earth, and there is nothing that can change that for better or worse" (p. 24). In his own case, Frank was "born into an ordinary, modern existence in 1945, an only child to decent parents of no irregular point of view, no particular sense of their *place* [Ford's italics] in history's continuum, just two people afloat on the world and expectant like most others in time, without a daunting conviction about their own consequence" (p. 24). His father, Frank goes on to say, played golf a lot and died when Frank was fourteen. Frank was sent off to military school on the Mississippi Gulf Coast and went home on holidays "to my mother's bungalow in Biloxi, and occasionally I saw her brother Ted" who took him on trips to Mobile and Pensacola but was not close to him. His mother remarried and moved to Skokie, Illinois, to live with her second husband, and after that, while Frank was at the University of Michigan, his mother treated him "like a nephew she didn't know very well, and who worried her, even though she liked me" (p. 28). She then got cancer and died.

Such a family is hardly the Compsons or the Gants or the Fairchilds, or even the families of any number of contemporary southern writers. Frank has no conscious ancestral past, no family burden, not only no grandfathers but no brothers and sisters, no cousins—no cousins, that is, until the end of the story when he happens to run into some in Florida: "Since coming here the surprise is that I have had the chance to touch base with honest-to-goodness relatives, some cousins of my father's who wrote me . . . to say that a Great-Uncle Eulice had died in California, and that they would like to see me if I was ever in Florida. Of course, I didn't know them and doubt I had ever heard their names. But I'm glad that I have now, as they are genuine salt of the earth" (p. 370). His cousin, Buster Bascombe, tells Frank about his father, and Frank realizes, "I hardly remember my father, and so it is all news to me, news even that *anyone* knew him" (p. 371).

This, then, is our unburdened Southerner. And not only do family and past mean nothing to him, the South and his identity as Southerner, he insists, mean nothing to him either. The South of his remembrance—and this is Mississippi, remember—isn't mysterious, isn't violent, isn't savage, isn't racially benighted, isn't Gothic or grotesque, isn't even *interesting*. In fact, it is not the South that fascinates Frank but—and this will be a shock to those steeped in American regional distinctiveness or lack of it —it is the Middle West that is fascinating, and what Frank constructs is not a Southern Mystique but a kind of Midwestern one. It is the American Heartland, then, the much maligned Midwest, the target of much of Walker Percy's satire—to the traditional southern imagination, the tasteless, standardized, materialistic, and just plain boring Midwest—that this ex-Southerner is drawn to. Not the mind of the South he explores, but the mind of the Middle West: it is a practical, matter-of-fact, things-in-order kind of place, a land which finds reality in things, not in ideas—a land populated, Frank discovers, with Barbs and Marges and Sues, where there is available "anything-you-want-within-sensible-limits." In Detroit he reflects, "I have read that with enough time American civilization will make the midwest of any place, New York included. And from here that seems not at all bad. Here is a great place to be in love; to get a land-grant education; to own a mortgage; to see a game under the lights" (p. 115). Even the midwestern accent—sharpened vowels, the dropped definite articles—fascinates Frank. And he approaches everything midwestern, as he approaches the suburban, middle-class culture of New Jersey, without distancing himself, without condescension.

Here we have, then, the southern expatriate for the eighties, with no interest in past, place, family, religion, community, guilt, and burdens of history, family or regional or otherwise. Or do we? It should be obvious by this point that, indeed, we do not—that the more Frank protests he is not interested in the past, in family, in place, and in the South, the more we are convinced that he is; and so, despite his own lack of storied past, distinguished family, and fixed place, is his creator, Ford. Frank's great interest in the *absence* of past, of historical burden, of family heritage, of fixed place, of community suggests a southern mind that is fascinated by these things. A true disregard of place, of history, would require an unconsciousness of it, and Frank has anything but that. Even the midwestern mind, as he defines it, is made up of qualities that are, conspicuously, *not* southern. Frank's is hardly the case of that other Mississippian in the Northeast three-quarters of a century before, Quentin at Harvard, saying of the South, "I dont hate it. I dont. I dont,"[6] but it *is* Frank Bascombe—who resembles in so many ways his creator—saying "I'm not at all interested in the South. I'm not. I'm not." One recalls, more than incidentally, that Quentin's mother's maiden name was also Bascomb, a fact that would not have been lost on Ford, who, as we have seen, knew Faulkner's work very well. Frank Bascombe, then, is, quite literally, a cousin of Quentin Compson—though a distant one, in another place far removed from Mississippi.[7] In any case—to return to my larger argument—if we read *The Sportswriter* closely we find that Frank, and Ford, are very much interested in the South, in matters that are at the heart of the southern experience; and also that the narrative voice is a particular kind of southern voice, and that Ford is very much, as we shall see, within a particular southern literary tradition.

But, first, to return to place: Despite having no tie to a postage stamp of soil in northern Mississippi or a plantation in the Delta or a farm in Tennessee—and despite being the creation of an author who professes little faith in traditional ideas of place—Frank Bascombe nonetheless is keenly attuned to place. Although he calls himself "a man with no place to go in particular" (p. 338), wherever he goes—and he is indeed on the move—he has a great desire, nearly a compulsion, to link with place, whether the place is suburban New Jersey or Detroit: a great sensitivity to where things are, what happened there, and what they meant.[8] We see this in particular in his detailed description of Haddam, the New Jersey commuter town in which he has lived for fourteen years —not the Haddam in Connecticut of Wallace Stevens's poem "Thirteen Ways of Looking at a Blackbird," but there is some evidence that Ford had Stevens's Haddam in mind. Frank is indeed one of the "thin men of Haddam" of Stevens's poem, one of the overly cerebral men, and Ford's novel, like the poem, is about ways of seeing, ways of perceiving.[9]

Just as Ford does not disregard place, neither does he neglect family and religion, as might appear to be the case. Family, in fact, is at the center of the novel, although a new kind of family. Frank and his former wife, known only as X, are divorced but still are linked, both through their grief over the death of their son Ralph and in their love for their two remaining children. Frank, who lives in the house they once had shared, sometimes comes to X's house, sits outside in his car, and looks. Further, at the end of the novel, he decides—in a setting not given to such discoveries in most southern novels, and a scene that almost parodies the idea of southern family—that to have an ancestral history, an extended family, even if an unfamiliar one, is not such a bad thing after all. After visiting his new-found relatives, the Buster Bascombes, in Florida, Frank concludes:

> And, truthfully, when I drive back up Highway 24 just as the light is falling beyond my condo, behind its wide avenue of date palms and lamposts, I am usually (if only momentarily) glad to have a past, even an imputed and remote one. There is something to that. It is not a burden, though I've always thought of it as one. I cannot say that we all need a past in full literary fashion, or that one is much useful in the end. But a small one doesn't hurt, especially if you're already in a life of your own choosing. [p. 371]

One could point to other ways in which Frank is more southern than he professes—in particular, his rage against abstraction or rationalism and his love of mystery. His announced preference for the supernatural, the unknown, in religion—his distaste for "factualists" (p. 204) or rationalists—is not very different from John Crowe Ransom's distaste for rationalism in his book *God Without Thunder* (1930), and Frank's protests of those who analyze and categorize, who explain too much ("anti-mystery types down to the core," he calls them), could have been uttered by Donald Davidson in his harangue against sociologists. "Some things can't be explained," Frank says. "They just are" (p. 233).

These and other traditional southern concerns could be explored. So could further elements of parody of things southern. Not only does Ford have his ex-Southerner discover his roots in a south Florida stucco bungalow (rather than, say, in Faulkner fashion, in the yellowed ledgers of an old plantation commissary), have him find that the current bearer of family honor is a retired railroad brakeman, "the salt of the earth," named Buster (a far cry from Jason Lycurgus and Quentin MacLachan), have him find religion, as Buster also does, in a palmist (rather than in a thundering Calvinist church or in the Big Woods), have him, at that, find only a "small" past (not one in "full literary fashion"), but Ford, in looking back on Frank's college days, has him describe the novel he had begun when he decided to be a writer, a novel nearly a parody of the usual racially charged, Christ-haunted southern production. It was the story of a young Southerner trying to reconcile present with guilty past, being initiated by a series of adventures including "a violent tryst with a Methodist minister's wife who seduces him in an abandoned slave-quarters" (and what else, in one respect, was the postbellum South *but* "abandoned slave-quarters"?). The manuscript, Frank tells us, was "lost in the mail": "I hadn't kept a copy" (p. 36).

Indeed, *The Sportswriter* itself is, among other things, a commentary on the traditional southern novel. It is not accidental that Frank's lone companion in his spacious home in Haddam is "a six-foot-five-inch Negro," an African student at the local seminary and a "stern-faced apologist for limitless faith" (p. 30) who lives in the attic: Frank knows he is there, hears him, and feels a certain comfort in his presence. Other allusions to the southern past or to southern literature present themselves. I have spoken of Frank Bascombe's kinship, however improbable, with Quentin Compson. One must note, in other ways, Ford's sly and clever use of *The Sound and the Fury*. Not only is Ford's protagonist given Quentin's mother's name—and this novel, like Faulkner's, a story of family dissolution—but it begins on Good Friday and takes place on Easter weekend, as *The Sound and the Fury* does, and contains numerous symbols of death and resurrection. Further, Ralph Bascombe's birthday, over Easter weekend, is also the birthday of Faulkner's Benjy—whose original name was Maury, named for his uncle Maury Bascomb.

There is no particular system at work in all this. Rather, there are sly and nearly hidden references to any number of literary works, southern and nonsouthern, in *The Sportswriter*, and I would guess if one asked Ford about them he would say, as Faulkner used to, that he didn't even know they were there, and certainly meant nothing by them. One finds allusions not only to Wallace Stevens but also T. S. Eliot ("The Hollow Men") and Theodore Roethke ("First Meditation") as well. At other times one is reminded of Melville. "My name is Frank Bascombe" (p. 3), the novel begins, echoing the first sentence of *Moby Dick*. "And I am still here to tell about it," Bascombe, like Ishmael the survivor—and a Presbyterian, like Ishmael, whose companion is a giant black man—goes on to say (p. 4). ("And I only am escaped alone to tell thee," Melville, quoting *Job*, begins Ishmael's Epilogue.) Indeed, Bascombe's given name is as full of possibilities as his Christian one. *I am Frank*, he tells us, but in fact he is anything but frank, anything but candid and reliable. This book of "truth-telling," as the *New York Magazine* called it,[10] is in fact, on one level, a book of great prevarication; to be more precise, the narrator is factually reliable but emotionally unreliable. He calls himself a happy man, he insists he is a happy man, but like his ancestor Quentin he protests too much.

One hesitates to carry all this further, and I would not if Ford did not slyly ask for it, but giving his sportswriter the name Frank is doubly curious. For who was America's most notable sportswriter at the time Ford wrote but another Frank, named Deford. And our hero shares a great deal in common with Frank Deford —another with-it, sensitive, attractive man who writes in-depth human interest stories for a slick sports magazine (Deford, at the time, for *Sports Illustrated*), had also written a best-selling novel (*Everybody's All-American*) for which he sold movie rights, and had endured the death of his child. One finds other suggestions that Ford, heeding in his novel contemporary popular writers as well as canonical ones, has created such a Frank—a Frank, that is, created by [Richard] Ford, Frank *of* Ford, Frank *De*ford. With any other novelist, I repeat, I might pass up the evidence, resist the temptation, but not with our subject, an especially cunning and slippery sort.

Indeed, we could discuss *The Sportswriter* as a particular expression of the postmodern imagination, a novel about writing for writers, a work of literature which is among other things a rejection of "literature," which, as Frank Bascombe tells us, teaches us "lies" (p. 16). (*Sports*writing, on the other hand, which teaches us "that there are no transcendent themes in life," is more to be trusted.) But rather than pursue those directions further, I wanted to return to this novel as a particular kind of *southern* novel, to turn to a particular southern literary tradition in which, I believe, it is possible to place *The Sportswriter*. Ford has written something of tradition and literary influences in an essay, "The Three Kings," in *Esquire* in 1983. Two of the three kings, the three writers whose influence he has felt, I have already mentioned—Faulkner and Hemingway. The third is Fitzgerald. But he does not here, nor does he anywhere else as far as I can determine, mention the writer whose work this novel most closely resembles —Walker Percy. For Frank Bascombe in *The Sportswriter* has a *voice* very much like Binx Bolling's in *The Moviegoer;* or, I should say, is a combination of Binx's voice and that of an earlier southern wanderer, Jack Burden in *All the King's Men.*

Frank Bascombe, that is, is another in that line of reflective and somewhat paralyzed well-bred, well-mannered, and well-educated young southern white males who tell their stories in the first person and are moved by the need to connect. (One finds other such examples in Allen Tate's Lacy Buchan in *The Fathers* and Peter Taylor's Phillip Carver in *A Summons to Memphis.*) Like Jack Burden and, especially, Binx, Frank is philosophical in a casual sort of way, a facile sort of way, fond of self-mockery, and given to inventing or appropriating terms to explain himself and his view of the world. Jack Burden, of course, explains his own conduct and that of others in terms of what he calls the Great Sleep and the Great Twitch; Percy, drawing on Kierkegaard and other thinkers, lets Binx talk about everydayness, certification, rotation, repetition, and the "Little Way." Frank has read his Kierkegaard as well—or his Percy. His creed of forgetting that we encountered earlier—"I am a proponent of . . . forgetting. . . . There is no hope unless we can forget"—comes straight from the epigraph to Percy's *The Last Gentleman,* Kierkegaard's "If a man cannot forget, he will never amount to much" (*Either/Or*). And Frank, as well, is in the habit of devising *his* terms—dreaminess, literalism, factualism, relenting—to explain his states of mind and those of others. Dreaminess he defines as "a state of suspended recognition and a response to too much useless and complicated factuality. Its symptoms can be a long-term interest in the weather, or a sustained soaring feeling, or a bout of the stares that you sometimes can not even know about except in retrospect" (p. 42). Dreaminess results in paralysis, in getting nothing accomplished—operating somewhat like the fugue states of Percy's Will

Barrett in *The Last Gentleman* or, even more, like Jack Burden's Great Sleep—and it occurs in Frank's life, as in Jack's, just before the breakup of his marriage. Frank resembles Jack in other ways. He is a writer who cannot write, fleeing from his novel-in-progress just as Jack flees from his dissertation. He tells his story, as Jack does, in a series of flashbacks which bring us finally back to the present. And when his son dies, he responds in Jack Burden fashion. When life becomes too tangled back East, Jack says, "when you don't like it where you are, you always go west,"[11] and this is precisely what Frank himself does. Immediately after his son's burial, he takes off alone in his car, heading west. Unlike Jack, he can't make it all the way to the coast. He turns around and heads back to New Jersey—and dreaminess.

Frank calls himself a literalist, by which he means "a man [who] will enjoy an afternoon watching people while stranded in an airport in Chicago, while a factualist can't stop worrying why his plane was late out of Salt Lake, and gauging whether they'll still serve dinner or just a snack" (pp. 132–33). A literalist, then, is more engaged in the moment, more accepting, thinking more concretely. A literalist—that is, Frank—cannot abide "idiotic factualism or the indignity of endless explanation" (p. 206). One wonders if Frank is as much of a literalist as he contends—what else is his story in *The Sportswriter* but an act of explaining, of making himself clear—but in expressing his strong *distaste* for factualism and in embracing literalism he is expressing nothing more than the presumed southern abhorrence of abstraction and preference for the concrete.

It is not only the casual philosophizing, however, that links Frank with Jack Burden and, in particular, Binx Bolling. Nor is it just the similar roles Binx and Frank play, the one—as the title announces—a moviegoer, the other a sportswriter. Both are watchers: one watches movies, the other watches sports. Each is essentially passive. But beyond that, it is the tone, the language, the cadences, the detailed social observation, the attention to southern *types* that links Ford with Percy. The ex-Southerner Frank has as keen an eye for varieties of the southern species as Percy's Binx—for instance, his description of his Vanderbilt-educated internist in New Jersey, Fincher Barksdale, who

> is the kind of Southerner who will only address you through a web of deep and antic southernness, and who assumes everybody in earshot knows all about his parents and history and wants to hear an update on them at every opportunity. . . . The perfect Southerner-in-exile, a slew-footed main-street change-jangler. . . . At Vandy he was the tallish, bookish Memphian meant for a wider world. . . . At Hopkins he met and married a girl from Goucher who couldn't stand the South and craved the suburbs." [pp. 68–69][12]

All this is not necessarily to say that Ford, any more than Barry Hannah, is Percy for the eighties, Percy for expatriates, a post-Christian Percy, but it is to suggest that Ford, too, is in a tradition, and, at least in *The Sportswriter*, it is not principally the tradition of Faulkner, or of his other kings, Hemingway or Fitzgerald. Rather, antecedents move up a generation. Not Faulkner and Wolfe but Percy and—in the cases of certain other contemporary writers—Welty and O'Connor are influences: the second generation of modern southern writers are now literary ancestors themselves. There is much more one could say about *The Sportswriter*, particularly how this novel, which is so much like *The Moviegoer* in certain ways, is so very different in others. But I will stop here. Suffice it to say that in *The Sportswriter* Ford, the presumed ex-Southerner, has written a book about New Jersey that is very much a book about the South. He has written a southern novel in a southern tradition, a non-Faulkner tradition, in spite of himself. Or perhaps not in spite of himself at all. Rather, cleverly, slyly, he may have written a southern novel that he knew was southern all along. He is modern, close to postmodern, but he is —to borrow a term from John Crowe Ransom—modern with the southern accent.

2

Josephine Humphreys, by birth and background, fits more naturally into Walker Percy's world than does Richard Ford. A native of Charleston, as we have seen—of old Charleston, the great-great-granddaughter of the secretary of the treasury of the Confederacy—she studied at Duke University with Reynolds Price and (like William Styron, Fred Chappell, Anne Tyler, and Price himself) with William Blackburn. After graduate work in English at Yale and the University of Texas, she married, returned to Charleston, had two sons, taught briefly, and did not publish her first novel until she was nearly forty.[13] That novel, *Dreams of Sleep* (1984), and her other work, *Rich in Love* (1987), are set in and around Charleston, but they could have been set in certain other places in the coastal South where the world of old families and traditional southern values comes into conflict with a faith in the sufficiency of present and future. *Rich in Love*, which takes place in the Charleston suburb of Mount Pleasant, seems to be standard, though unusually well written, contemporary southern fare—seen from the point of view of another teenaged girl—in which wife leaves prosperous husband, husband takes up with hair stylist, and daughter comes home married and pregnant, while around them a New South of wealth and leisure is being created and their black friend's daughter gets a scholarship to Duke's summer program for precocious seventh graders. It is a wise book, in its way a reflection on history, but an unpretentious book. This is Walker Percy's world seen through seventeen-year-old eyes, Barry Hannah's without violence and madness.

But it is *Dreams of Sleep*, Humphreys's first novel, her finest and most rewarding, in which the influence of Percy is most clearly detected. Perhaps no other recent novel by a younger writer holds in better balance the interests of the contemporary South and those of its predecessor, and none is more concerned with the relationship between the two. Its characters, Will and Alice Reese and their friends and acquaintances, have their being in a world of mass culture—thirty-three-year-old Alice "still knows the rock groups, the names of the singers and the words of the songs," and another character takes meals at Wendy's, Popeye's, and Arby's but prefers Hardee's because "I feel at home there"[14]—but this novel, set in Charleston, not outside it, cannot help meditating on time, change, futurity, the relationships between North and South, self and community, men and women, money and history. A novel of conscious social commentary of the sort usually associated with southern male authors, from Mark Twain through Percy to Richard Ford, it contains the same sort of semi-serious, sometimes hilarious self-conscious regionalism, southern and otherwise, we find especially in Percy. After an interlude for Ford's impassioned, if suspect, defense of the Middle West, with Humphreys it's back to the old Ohio-bashing. Percy pokes fun at "chicken-shit Ohioans," driving their Airstream trailers to Florida, saying "Kerrell" for Carol, "mear" for mirror, "tock" for talk, and "he and I" in the objective case; Hannah holds forth on "Ohio. . . . the worst state in the union . . . Ohio is silly. . . . DROP THE BIG ONE ON OHIO."[15] And Humphreys joins the chorus:

> What Will has against Duncan [his stepfather] is . . . that he came from Ohio. Ohioans love what they think is the South. Boiled shrimp, debutantes, the Civil War. . . . And now they are not only vacationing here. They're buying condos. They're staying year-round and investing in real estate, restaurants, inns, banks; buying up farmland as if the South

> were some non-English-speaking banana republic crying for development in the image of Ohio. . . .
>
> But the New South is Ohio warmed over. No one will know until Ohioans have insinuated themselves into key positions in the business community, and it will be too late. [p. 47]

What do all these people have against Ohio, a worthy citizen of the Buckeye State might wonder if he reads much southern fiction these days. Too much sameness and too much saneness, Percy, Humphreys, Hannah, and other Southerners of rarefied tastes might answer. In fact I, like Frank Bascombe, rather like Ohio, its orderly farms and rusting cities and meadows by the banks of the Olentangy, but that's beside the point. The point is that poking fun at Ohio seems to have become a staple of contemporary southern fiction, and since southern scholars these days make it a practice to categorize and classify southern writers into schools and traditions, I might suggest as such a category the Ohio-Bashing School of Southern Fiction.

But Humphreys not only writes a novel of clever satire, but in *Dreams of Sleep* comes close to the southern novel of ideas associated with Warren and Percy. Certain characters seem to be created at least in part to express ideas, for example Alice's newspaper-editor father, with his Princeton degree in philosophy and his skepticism about progress: "Her father said the world was not improving: what looks like progress is only change" (p. 135). Other characters stop themselves in the midst of everyday tasks and think thoughts of the sort associated with Percy characters: "Who can be sad in a supermarket, with all its proof of human omnipotence?" (p. 136); or "Why do philosophers in the South so often end up as newspapermen, poets as doctors?" (p. 136); or "A house with a woman and children in it at dusk is frightening to the man who draws near and hears the muffled voices, those dishes being washed. The pure domestic horror of it rings down his spine" (p. 37).

Will and Alice Reese are young professionals, he a gynecologist, she a mathematician and currently full-time, if not altogether successful, mother to two daughters. The point of view in the novel shifts between Will and Alice, two solitaries for whom "love is not a natural state" (p. 231). The story begins and ends in Alice's mind: she has, on the one hand, a passion for order, a bent for abstraction not usually seen in southern women in fiction (has any previous character been a mathematician?), but she is, as well, a disordered and confused soul, aware of her husband's affair with his nurse–office manager, Claire, but paralyzed for action, deeply disappointed about life, obsessed with nothingness, nearly incapable (until the end) of hope. Thin, frail, disoriented, Alice yearns not, as one of her southern predecessors in marital unhappiness had, for an "awakening" (Humphreys' title, employing the same metaphor, although differently, seems an ironic twist on Kate Chopin's) but rather for the dreams of sleep, or escape, she once had had in abundance. She is hardly alone in contemporary southern fiction in being drawn to dreams; one finds it remarkable, in a post-Freudian age, to discover just how important dreams are in, among other works, *The Sportswriter,* Hannah's *Ray* and *The Tennis Handsome,* Gail Godwin's *The Finishing School,* Reynolds Price's *Good Hearts,* Fred Chappell's *I Am One of You Forever,* and Anne Tyler's *Dinner at the Homesick Restaurant*—not to mention Godwin's *Dream Children,* Jayne Anne Phillips's *Machine Dreams,* and Ellen Gilchrist's *In the Land of Dreamy Dreams.* It is not my purpose here, though, to explore this outbreak of dreams and what it says about the contemporary southern psyche. My concern is with Alice, whose dreams assume many forms—catastrophes, an unfed baby in a dresser drawer, hidden staircases to silent rooms—but in most cases involve a tension between responsibility and the sweetness of solitude. Even when awake, indeed, Alice is dreamy, "foggy."

Alice Reese is a well-drawn if rather elusive character, an "eerie [portrait] in passivity," as Ann Hulbert has described her.[16] But it is Will who is the more compelling character—the character Humphreys, perhaps in spite of herself, seems to be most interested in—and he is perhaps the most surely drawn male character by any contemporary southern woman writer. A man in that tradition we have already encountered of well-bred, overly cerebral southern males—from Faulkner's Quentin through Tate's Lacy Buchan, Warren's Jack Burden, and Percy's Binx Bolling and Will Barrett, to Lee Smith's Richard Burlage and Ford's Frank Bascombe—Will Reese is nonetheless an original creation. He is a somewhat less sympathetic character than any of the others (save, perhaps, Burlage), although, one feels, drawn fairly and accurately: Humphreys may specialize in Ohio-bashing but not male-bashing. Nonetheless, Will is a rather ill-spirited sort ("You are very mean, you know," his girlfriend says without malice), characterized more by his dislikes than his likes. A South Carolinian, he does not like South Carolina—"fat and flushed, oppressive" —preferring "dignified and masculine, intelligent" North Carolina instead (p. 38); yet after attending Chapel Hill, he returns to Charleston to live. A gynecologist, he does not like women. He once liked women, felt the women and babies he delivered were *his*, but later women didn't "[live] up to [his] expectations" (p. 102). That is, those same women were no longer young and fresh, healthy and problem-free. Neither does Will, *outside* the office and delivery room, think much of women, as his treatment both of Alice and his girlfriend, Claire, demonstrates.

Will is hardly, then, the affable, appealingly confused character Percy creates in Binx and Will Barrett, yet he shares much in common with them. His problem, like theirs, is difficult to diagnose, harder still to remedy, but it manifests itself in emptiness, loneliness, vulnerability (*his* dreams are often of public nakedness), and yearning, which he is able to stave off periodically by fixing his attention on an outside attraction: "He'd always had a nameless, unanchored longing; and when at critical points in his life, a period of intense longing coincided with the appearance of a suitable object, he fell for it head over heels, and believed he had discovered a great passion. Poetry, friendship, work, women—each at one time he'd held to be the center of his life" (p. 197). These movements toward temporary engagement—these attempts to avoid the abyss, or more often everydayness, through attachments, first to Alice, then his work, then Claire—come close to a Percy character's reliance on rotation, though they are not quite the same.[17] What Will knows about himself most of all, however, is that he is a profoundly *sad* man, and that sadness casts a shadow on all he sees, particularly—since he sees them more than anything else—women. He notices his office workers Cindy and Michelle coming in. They do not *seem* sad, young and married, "their voices high and carelessly mingling." But soon "a grimness sets into their faces, especially around the mouth. Their lips are tight against their teeth. And to Will, watching from the corridor, they are sad girls with no joy in their lives" (pp. 36–37). He notices the same sadness in Alice and Claire. Overall, the sadness of women "is oppressive, a general gloom raining down over the world. . . . They all seem sad—his patients, the nurses, the women driving Volvos through the streets, with sunglasses on their heads and sadness in their faces. What can you do when the women are like that?" (p. 34). Indeed, "the only woman he knows who is not sad" (p. 46) is his mother, Marcella, a million-dollar realtor for Dixie Homes who drives around Charleston in her Cadillac with a license plate reading REALTY.

Unlike Frank Bascombe, Will *knows* he is not a happy man, and he believes he knows at least part of the reason. Like Frank, and like Binx Bolling and Will Barrett, Will lost his father when he was young, and Will attributes much of what he has become to never having known his father. Who was this man, he asks, other than an Episcopalian who was not very good at making money? "What did he live for?" (p. 31). "Edmund Reese lived out his life without ever explaining himself. He never told his son where his treasure was" (p. 32). And he died early. It was the "sudden nature" of that death that left Will "with this terrible feeling of inconclusiveness, as if his father had been taken away before completing the work of fatherhood, leaving behind an unfinished product. He blamed his father's untimely death for all his own shortcomings, for his unsureness and his perverseness; all of it was Edmund's fault, for dying" (p. 55).

It was not all Edmund's fault, of course. Will exaggerates his father's impact on himself as surely as Frank Bascombe underestimates *his* father's impact. But Will is a man, unlike Frank, who makes it a habit to attribute even more to the past than probably belongs there. He runs counter altogether to the ahistorical cast of mind one encounters in most contemporary southern fiction, although his attitude toward history is highly ambiguous. To Alice, history is burden and little else: she looks enviously at her seventeen-year-old babysitter who is "unburdened by a sense of history or home or kin" (p. 129). Frank Bascombe would agree that that is ideal, and so, in certain respects, would Will. He prefers North Carolina to South Carolina, after all, partly because North Carolina represents the present, South Carolina the past. But he himself is descended from a family whose "history [goes] back to the Lords Proprietors" (p. 74) and in many respects, especially when the historic past is pitted against modern commercialism, Will comes down strongly on the side of the past. Alice, for all her fears, is open to change—changing houses, changing neighborhoods, a changing world. Will is not. On vacation at Sea Island with Alice and his daughters, he "couldn't stand" the manufactured happiness, "the pool and the women, the yellow umbrellas":

> He drove out to Bloody Marsh, where the Spanish were defeated and turned back, kept from moving north to Savannah and Charleston. He drove to Fort Frederica, the first English settlement in Georgia, of which nothing now remains but the brick outline of each house in the ground, like a life-size map laid out under the giant oaks at a bend in the Frederica River. He sat on the riverbank and got sunburned. "Those are real places," he said. "This"—the pool, the women, the yellow umbrellas—"is a fake place." [p. 76]

Will tries to bring himself—to *will* himself[18]—into a harmony with the historical past, yet he is one who belongs too surely to the fragmented present. The same week, at Sea Island, one night Alice awakens to hear him whispering, one assumes to Claire, on the phone.

Dreams of Sleep is a novel in which the present encroaches on the past—and, occasionally, vice versa—with particular insidiousness. Will recalls the morning of his father's funeral when, after a quarrel with his mother at breakfast, he had left the house and walked to the cemetery, passing through "a scrap-metal yard where rusting cars were piled six high": "Beyond the junkyard the old cemetery was hidden, a secret garden the developers had not been able to touch" (p. 168). It is close to being a metaphor for the contemporary South, a particularly vivid image of the machine (rusting cars) in the garden (the cemetery), the junkyard threatening to overtake the cemetery which contained "Confederates and statesmen and a poet or two" (p. 168). Will's father was to be buried in Old Magnolia, the Protestant section; his mother would ultimately claim the only other place left in the family plot. "Will would have to go out to one of the new cemeteries with flat bronze markers sunk deep enough into the earth so that a lawn mower could go right over them, the whole spread looking like a golf course" (p. 169). Such is Will's dispossession, his alienation from both family and past.

Indeed, what one finds in this novel is nearly another parody of the treasured southern notion of the past in the present, for the past in the present in Charleston, circa 1980, means such totems as an apartment complex named "The Old South," where Will's boyhood friend and college classmate Danny Cardozo lives. Humphreys describes in some detail the Old South apartments and an encounter one night between Will and Danny after Will has discovered his friend's involvement with Claire. The Old South is a decaying place across the river, "a place with a pool and plenty of hibachis" (p. 159), full of divorcees, junkies, and other people with fragmented lives. Once, Humphreys tells us, better people had lived in the Old South, but security had been nonexistent. Now a "tougher bunch" inhabits it, and a murder occurred on the premises last year. Will calls the complex a "shit hole" and accuses Danny of planning to bring Claire here to live, but Danny insists "It's much classier than it looks" (p. 161). Will, however, is in a combative mood and, after joining Danny in drinking a half-full fifth of Rebel Yell, he insults his old friend, who then slugs Will. They stage a rather pathetic fight, throwing one punch each before Danny lands in the pool and remains under water pretending to drown. After Will "saves" him, Danny launches into a drunken, self-pitying speech about always having been "a ghost to myself, a fake Jew, a poor imitation of a Southern gentleman" (p. 166). He then invites Will along for deer hunting the next morning and asks him to bring the bourbon.

All this happens in the Old South, and nearly all the ingredients of southern glory are here for the parodying: the hunt, the duel over a woman, southern honor and chivalry, deep male friendship, and Rebel Yell. The Old South has come to this: a decaying and violent place with no security, a misplaced sense of honor, and a whimpering "Southern gentleman." But it is hardly the only example in *Dreams of Sleep* of the debasement of the southern past when it is brought into the present. Even more illustrative is the theme park which Will's Ohio stepfather, Duncan Nesmith, plans in Charleston, drawing on Low Country history. As Nesmith describes it to Will, it will be "like Six Flags or Carowinds" but not like Disney World. "This will be much more low-key, more in tune with the environment and related to the historical traditions of the area." The theme will be "pirates. To tie in with the riverfront. We'll have a couple of pirate ships that actually go out, take people on the river, out to Drum Island, where we'll give them maps to dig for buried treasure. Everything will have the pirate theme. . . . It's a natural because there really were pirates here. One of them was hanged on the Battery. We plan to reenact it" (p. 178).

It is "natural" just as Al Cantrell's Ghostland in *Oral History* is natural, appearing to draw on what is organic and indigenous but in fact only producing an artificial version having nothing to do with the original. History becomes a commodity, just another means of exercising the profit motive, and Humphreys seems to be acutely aware of the connection between history and money. When Duncan says that the theme park is supported by "local money"—that, in fact, "the initial idea came from them"—Will can't believe him: "There is no Charleston man who'd put money into something like that." It is doubtless a sound investment, but "*no true son of this city* [Humphreys' italics] would back a goddamned pirate park right there on the river: Don't try to tell me it's local money. . . . It's money without history. It's cut loose, and roams, raids us. . . . It's cur-dog money . . . without honor" (pp. 181–82).

Just what constitutes money *with* history and honor Will doesn't explain further—presumably he means old wealth, Charleston wealth, money made on the backs of slaves and commoners in the South Carolina Low Country—but to him Duncan Nesmith's plan is further evidence that he is cut off not only from family and past but also from place. Duncan and the Ohioans had already taken over much of what had been his:

> Land that Will's father used to measure, marsh and mud flat, woods, coast, swamp, is falling to Duncan Nesmith to be filled or cut over, skinned of all real growth, the virgin cypress, the tangle of honeysuckle and jasmine, and then *landscaped.* With plants that didn't even grow here in Edmund's lifetime. Dwarf juniper! Spruce! There must be vast nurseries in Akron and Dayton raising strains that will transplant south. [p. 48]

Now they will drain the marshland and create the pirate park. And "they aren't even Yankees—the old enemy. They're good guys. Americans" (p. 48).

For all the occasional jocularity of tone there is, to repeat, a deep sadness in *Dreams of Sleep*, and much of the sadness is connected to the realities of time. Alice wants time to move faster, so overwhelming is its deliberate pace—although on rare occasions one finds a more conventional basis for her sadness in time's *rapid* pace, in mutability and loss: "This sweet milk is already turning, these eggs in their perfect shells already going slowly bad" (p. 137). Will's sadness, as regards time, is altogether in that traditional literary mode, manifesting itself in nearly Wolfean meditations on change and loss:

> It isn't that nothing is left. It is that what remains [of his life and marriage] is such an old sad ghost of the thing that used to be, and he can't bear lying down with the vestiges. Hasn't he been looking for the thing that used to be, looking for it in Claire, looking for it in every woman giving birth on that stainless-steel table, looking for it desperately and

> pathetically even in the unfinished faces of his own daughters? And now he knows it is not to be found whole again; it is scattered and dispersed, past reassembling; blown ashes. [p. 174]

"O Lost!" Will might well add, echoing that October voice of "masculine" North Carolina: the ghost, the cadences, the sentiments are all Thomas Wolfe's. This may be the early 1980s in the Sun Belt, but Will can't shake the old sadness over decay and loss. He sees it everywhere he looks, in things so insignificant as Claire's kitchen: "He grew up in a house with the same refrigerator in its kitchen for twenty years, same stove, sink, breadbox, can opener on the wall. Now a kitchen isn't good for more than five years, the styles change" (p. 114). And he sees loss in things so magnificent as the proud, spacious Charleston houses that have been carved into apartments. As evening falls, he meditates on one such structure in front of Claire's carriage house, "a tall Victorian mansion that has been cut up" into twelve units:

> Once this whole house was the home of one family. Is this how things fall apart, then? Not in sudden collapse, but by slow fragmentation. Houses turn into apartments, estates into subdivisions. We can't sustain the things we used to sustain: dynasties, clans, big families; we can't even maintain their monuments. Statues are losing their noses, tombstones their letters. [p. 111]

Dynasties, clans, families: these too are not as they once were, particularly in the American South, but in most respects Will has adjusted to that change better than to certain other changes. Granted, early in his marriage he had wanted a large family, "lots of children," but Alice's body, enduring three miscarriages, was "reluctant at every stage." And "the bodies of his [daughters] don't promise fecundity" either. "They are too thin." But this recognition causes Will regret only because "small families are feeble . . . in a big family affliction and grief are less destructive; they get diluted" (p. 52), *not* because, as was the case, say, with Thomas Sutpen as any number of earlier southern patriarchs, a small family—particularly one with no sons—precluded the possibility of dynasty. Primogeniture, honor, duty, dynasty: these have, in large measure, fled from the southern family novel in our time. Not once does Will regret he has *daughters;* not once does he regret that his *name* will not be passed on. Continuity in family is seen as a mixed blessing in any case: both Will and Alice are products of homes in which little love was given, and for Will "a dull succession of generations . . . has left . . . no spiritual legacy" (p. 104). Thus Will's regrets about family are not lofty, abstract; they are immediate and tangible. He wants to live happily in the present with what he has, to fight his way through what Michael Griffith has called "the minutae of daily life."[19]

Of greater concern to Will than family, more at the core of his sadness, seems to be the visible ravages of time, the surest lesson of history for this student of the past:

> Growing up in an old city, you learn history's one true lesson: that history fades. Nothing sticks together for very long without immense effort. His own strong house is in a constant process of disintegration. He calls workmen to come repair the roof, paint the porches, replace sills; but even this work has no permanence, it will have to be done again in four or five years. Is this noble activity for a man? Patching, gluing, temporizing, begging for time? [p. 112]

Given Will's melancholy, it is inevitable that his sadness about the loss and decay of the remote past—antebellum and Victorian mansions—will finally extend to a more accessible past, and it does. Nearly as much as for Mason's Samantha Hughes, although for vastly different reasons, for both Will and Alice the 1960s and early 1970s have already become "history." Indeed, Humphreys is a writer concerned not only with the individual drama but also with what might be called the condition of the South, and she attempts to paint a picture of a broad spectrum of Charleston life. She devotes a great deal of time to the babysitter Alice hires, a poor but lively white girl named Iris who lives in the now-black projects and whose best friend is a black boy. But Humphreys writing about the Charleston poor is like Dreiser writing about the established rich: very detailed and careful but not quite on target. She is much more convincing when she limits her point of view to Will or Alice, when she captures *their* distress over urban decay and racial tension, focuses on their belief that the South of even a decade ago is now long past, that a new, uncertain time has emerged. "What will happen to all these black people," Alice wonders, "now the movement is dead, their heroes tucked away in public offices? Was the whole civil rights movement nothing but a minor disturbance in the succession of years? White people have started telling jokes again" (p. 134). Will takes the past even further ahead, into the present, indeed looks *ahead* to looking back not at the decay of the Old South but this time at the decay of the New. "I've got a feeling," he tells Duncan Nesmith, "the boom is about over. The New South is about to age overnight like those children in the tabloids. I see empty hotels and abandoned villas and unthatched cabanas all over the Sun Belt. Rats scurrying through the deserted theme parks" (p. 179).

There is little love in the ruins Will envisions as he leaps ahead to view what will soon be history. And indeed that South that Will envisioned in the early eighties is already with us, on a minor scale, if we consider the abandoned water parks, the grass growing in the cracks of parking lots for never-used shopping malls in Oil Bust Louisiana and Texas. The "doozy of a racial war" (p. 179) that Will foresees may be no more likely now than it was then, but both he and Alice recognize well that the euphoria of the immediate post-civil-rights era, the period of self-congratulations at having come through, the vision of a problem-free South which would find in the shining towers of Atlanta a new version of the City on a Hill—that *this* South, in its self-assurance and its innocence, is already past, is already history. Humphreys is indeed in the tradition of Walker Percy, is in this novel a most wise and nearly prophetic writer. *Dreams of Sleep* is a work that will have to be taken into account when, already looking ahead as Will Reese does, we look *back* at the Sun Belt, only that newest of New Souths.

4

Contemporary Southern Fiction and the Autochthonous Ideal

It should be clear by this point that these remarks hardly constitute an inclusive, much less a definitive study of contemporary southern fiction, or even such a study of those writers born since 1940. One of the hazards of undertaking an inquiry such as this is that all the returns are not yet in, and thus whatever I say will constitute—as George B. Tindall once entitled an essay about biography still in the making—a "preliminary estimate."[1] And not even fully that, since one is prevented by time and space from discussing certain other writers who are, even at this point, demonstrably as talented and as important as those under consideration. For in the South of 1990 that dream of poor southern book editors and apologists of the 1920s, responding to Mencken's "Sahara of the Bozart," has finally been realized. There *are*, this time, significant numbers of young southern writers one could claim—with truth, integrity, and no sectional bias—as among the nation's finest. The wise observer might hesitate to name names if he or she recalled another lesson from the 1920s and early 1930s, for if a scholar of southern literature in, say, 1930 had been asked to choose the leading southern fiction writers of the previous decade—those whose work would last—he would likely have chosen T. S.

Stribling, James Branch Cabell, Dubose Heyward, Julia Peterkin, Frances Newman, and possibly Thomas Wolfe, whose *Look Homeward, Angel* had just appeared. But he likely would not have chosen William Faulkner, author of four novels, including *The Sound and the Fury*. The only course in the face of such a history of southern literary prophecy is to ignore it altogether and take the plunge anyway, always keeping in mind the response Mencken customarily gave those readers who wrote him challenging his facts and prejudices: "It is possible, sir [or madam], that you may be right."

Thus certain other writers must be discussed, if only briefly, and if only to suggest that some of the concerns of contemporary southern fiction I have examined are not unique to those novelists on whom I have focused. Many other writers who set their work squarely in their world, our world, of commercial mass culture also might be seen in relation, often see themselves in relation, to the southern literary tradition, if sometimes, like Richard Ford, parodying that tradition.[2] We can safely say that *most* under-fifty southern writers—such as Anne Tyler, Alice Walker, Jayne Anne Phillips, Clyde Edgerton, Padgett Powell, Jill McCorkle, and Kaye Gibbons—are still more concerned with family than are most nonsouthern American writers, even if sometimes in a quirky and nontraditional manner; and that most of these writers are more concerned with community than most young nonsouthern writers. Anne Tyler's fiction serves as an example. After setting her first three novels in North Carolina, her childhood home, Tyler has placed nearly all of her fiction since in her adopted home, Baltimore, that curious city, above the Potomac but below the Mason-Dixon line, once considered southern but with far less southern identity now.[3] Tyler considers *herself* a southern writer, however: Welty was her greatest early influence, and considering the kind of half-amusing, eccentric figures she creates, one would think at times that she has picked up Welty's characters from rural Mississippi, changed their accents, and moved them to Maryland. Family is Tyler's great subject, and we find in the treatment of family, community, and religion in her fiction nearly parodies of traditional southern treatments. There is pathos in the desperate attempts of Ezra Tull in *Dinner at the Homesick Restaurant* and Maggie Moran in *Breathing Lessons* to sustain family and community, but there is also humor. Ezra's restaurant indeed becomes an attempt to achieve community in the midst of the fragmentation that is always Tyler's fictional world, but it is not a successful attempt. Diners come and go with no sense of continuity or allegiance to the place, the kitchen staff changes, the menu varies nightly, and the Tull family never manages to complete a meal together. The Tulls are bound together not through love but rather through an inability to forgive and to overcome resentment. The father, Beck, abandons his family when the children are young, not to return until his wife's funeral thirty-five years later. The mother, Pearl, is eulogized by the minister at her funeral as "a pillar of the community," yet as Tyler goes on to tell us, "she'd never shown the faintest interest in her community." As for religion, Pearl "was not at all religious, hadn't set foot in this church for decades." Tyler views that other great concern of southern novelists from Faulkner and Wolfe to Warren and Styron—time—with equal irreverence. Although Pearl's oldest son, Cody, waxes eloquent occasionally on the subjects of mutability and loss, the great romantic themes, professionally he is an efficiency expert: "Time is my obsession: not to waste it, not to lose it."[4]

Tyler is hardly the only contemporary southern writer who approaches familiar subjects in new ways. As Linda Wagner-Martin notes, Jill McCorkle begins her novel *Tending to Virginia* (1987) with a genealogy, reminiscent of such genealogies Faulkner included with some of his work—except, unlike Faulkner's patriarchal genealogy, this one is essentially matriarchal.[5]

McCorkle's treatment of community is equally revealing—not a community of white Southerners embracing or rejecting outsiders at will as in, say, *Light in August;* nor the spirit of community of men in the woods as in *The Bear;* but rather a community nearly exclusively of women. We find essentially the same idea of community in Lee Smith's *Black Mountain Breakdown* and *Fair and Tender Ladies* and, at least until the conclusion, in Alice Walker's *The Color Purple*. Like all communities, these are grounded in shared experiences and shared hurts, and like all communities these identify their pariahs—in both *Tending to Virginia* and, especially, *The Color Purple,* men. Men are those "others" who abuse (Albert, the wife beater in *The Color Purple;* Virginia's Uncle Raymond, the child molester), mystify, and often reject. Indeed, these novels and others written by women call into question the entire concept and role of that celebrated sense of community in traditional southern life and letters. To what extent did the traditional idea of community depend on hierarchy, each man in his place, each woman in hers? If that is the case, traditional ideas of community, like those of family, break down in an age in which place—gender role—is no longer so clearly defined. As Iris in Bobbie Ann Mason's story "Drawing Names" says to her grandfather, "Times are different now, Pappy. We're just as good as the men."[6]

In many other areas, however, we find a great deal of continuity in contemporary southern fiction. We find it in southern humor, not only Barry Hannah's zany and raucous brand but also Clyde Edgerton's finely crafted, kinder, gentler variety in *Raney* (1985) and other works, and, in still another vein, James Wilcox's social satire in *Modern Baptists* (1983) and *North Gladiola* (1985), novels nearly in the tradition of T. S. Stribling and the 1920s satirists. One also finds isolated attempts, in a novelist such as T. R. Pearson, to write a kind of fiction that reviewers find reminiscent of Faulkner (although Pearson's is perhaps even more reminiscent of Laurence Sterne). And we find any number of contemporary renderings of *Huckleberry Finn*, usually but not always with a different voice, often a different gender. One considers, first, Simons Manigault in Padgett Powell's *Edisto* (1984), a free-spirited twelve-year-old boy in the South Carolina low country who sheds his father and finds a more appealing substitute in a young (possibly black) man who becomes both friend and counselor and helps him see through false gods. But I am thinking even more of numerous female characters who serve as contemporary Huck Finns, an occurrence not altogether new in southern fiction (what else was Mick Kelly in Carson McCullers's *The Heart Is a Lonely Hunter*?) but one currently striking in its frequency. I think of Mason's Sam Hughes as well as McCorkle's Jo Spencer in *The Cheer Leader* (1984) ("It was a bad thing to do and since I hid it from the world, that made me a lying hypocrite and that was even better. I could be both good and bad"),[7] two teenaged girls with cross-gender names. I think of seventeen-year-old Lucille Odom, the independent-minded narrator of Josephine Humphreys's *Rich in Love* (1987); Beverly Lowry's independent, illegitimate Emma Blue, who lives in a trailer outside town (*Emma Blue*, 1978); or even Clyde Edgerton's free-spirited young woman, Raney, a somewhat older version of Huck. I think most of all of Kaye Gibbons's novel *Ellen Foster* (1987), a story told first person by a poor, downtrodden eleven-year-old white girl who becomes an orphan when her father drinks "his own self to death," and whose best friend is black: *Huckleberry Finn* a century later nearly to the year, updated and with a sex change and, in fact, not at all derivative as this description would suggest—another triumph of vernacular voice and tone.

What does it say that most Huck Finns in contemporary southern fiction are female? What does it suggest that women write novels in which men seem to be excluded from community? Perhaps, to entertain a possibility, that the writers themselves are sorts of Huck Finns, finding it difficult to accept received values, old notions of honor and hierarchy, or—as Huck called Tom's romantic ideas and schemes—"Tom Sawyer's lies." Most earlier fiction written by southern women, as I have suggested, had a somewhat different cast to it than fiction written by the most notable southern male writers, Faulkner, Wolfe, Warren, Ellison, Styron, and Percy. I have spoken earlier of the southern novel of ideas and conscious social commentary as having been principally a male domain, whose finest twentieth-century practitioner was Percy. And it might be added that the "big novel" to which I alluded in the beginning—the ambitious novel, that work concerned with the sweep of history or with the public arena, or both—has also in the South generally (with an exception such as *Gone with the Wind*) been undertaken by male authors: Faulkner, Wolfe, Warren, Ellison, and Styron. Whether this is because the male, particularly in southern society, was usually conditioned to think more ambitiously, that is, to ponder history and politics in which *he*, after all, could more easily participate—or whether it is because the vision of the male writer has tended for other reasons to be more abstract, less attentive to everyday truths and concrete details than that of most women writers—is debatable. I tend to think it is something of both. But a development of some interest and, I believe, consequence in the 1980s was that the *kinds* of novels written by southern men and those by southern women were no longer so easy to distinguish. As we have seen, Josephine Humphreys in *Dreams of Sleep* writes a novel of social commentary, nearly a novel of ideas in the Percy tradition. And certain contemporary southern male writers—one thinks of Clyde Edgerton and, over a longer period, Reynolds Price—demonstrate precisely that concrete vision, that eye for the particular, the small truth, that one earlier might have identified with women writers: they seem, that is, more nearly apostles of Welty than of Faulkner.

We find significant changes in southern fiction, then, reflecting larger changes in society as far as gender, family, and community are concerned. Indeed, some students of southern literature contend, the only thing that one can claim with confidence is still southern about southern fiction, and will continue to be distinctive, is *voice,* although I would tend to question that. It is indeed true, if we consider younger writers like Lee Smith, Edgerton, Gibbons, and McCorkle, that the voice in *that* fiction is distinctive, and distinctively southern. But Anne Tyler's voice is not "southern" in the same way, nor is Mason's, nor Richard Ford's, nor Padgett Powell's, and if we place too much emphasis on voice we are in danger of falling, if in a different way, into the old southern habit of assuming what is true of much southern fiction is true of all—with the result that if the young Southerner is going to "write," that Southerner feels that he or she must write in a particular voice.

There are other concerns for the contemporary southern writer, young or not, including one which the Agrarian critic and poet Donald Davidson detected for the southern writer of *his* time some sixty years ago. That is, according to Davidson, the Southerner, if he is not careful, is always in danger of becoming too much the self-conscious regionalist, one who begins with the recognition that he or she is primarily a "southern writer" with an opportunity and obligation to present or interpret Southerners to the rest of the nation—an intent that can result either in creating regional "types" (that is, local color) or can manifest itself in an excessive desire to explain (that is, a sort of sociological or reforming fiction).[8] The dangers to which Davidson alerted southern writers in the 1920s and 1930s are not quite so great today: as a species, Southerners are now somewhat better known and thus not so much to be gawked at, and few writers are out to reform the South any more. Percy, the most notable of southern "social commentators" among novelists, has also been among the South's finest storytellers.

But we might still consider what Davidson wrote, and consider further a particular standard for southern fiction, growing out of his concerns about explaining and interpreting, which he put forth in the late 1920s—what Davidson called the autochthonous ideal. By that term he meant a condition in which the writer was in a certain harmony with his social and cultural environment, was nearly *unconscious* of it as a "special" environment, quaint or rustic or backward, and thus was not motivated by any urge to interpret or explain.[9] Davidson's reasons for proposing an autochthonous ideal were not so artistically pure as they might seem: he felt, especially in the climate of the 1920s, that to recognize the South as different, to call attention to its aberrations, was also to analyze, criticize, and eventually reform it. As an upholder of the racial status quo and other manifestations of the southern status quo, he did not *want* too much attention to be paid to the region's various peculiar institutions, at least not by those he considered the wrong people. And just as his reasons for upholding such an ideal for southern fiction were suspect, the artistic consequences of such a standard would not always be favorable. For Davidson was essentially calling for a lack of social *tension* between the literary artist and his social and cultural environment, and it is out of tension, not harmony, that great art often arises.

But having said this—recognizing Davidson's purposes, his dubious social philosophy and reactionary political views—I must also say that his point, as concerns the matter of fiction, has some merit. That writer, indeed, suffers as a craftsman, a storyteller, when he is overly concerned with presenting, interpreting, explaining. He tends to tell rather than to show, to focus on southern folkways and idiosyncrasies, on what is distinctive in the region, not what is universal in man. He is in some danger, that is, of dealing in generalities, not particularities as the best fiction writers must.

One of Davidson's concerns need not detain us—to repeat,

few southern writers today are out to reform the South—but the other must, for the contemporary writer is indeed in danger of writing a sort of twentieth-century local color. One thinks of such writers as Ellen Gilchrist, Beverly Lowry, and James Wilcox, who, although abundantly talented, sometimes give in to southern stereotypes. Other writers such as Lee Smith might sometimes seem to stray in that direction, but Smith well recognizes the perils of focusing on regional types rather than individuals. What else is her portrait of Jennifer in *Oral History* but a recognition of that tendency to categorize and classify? The writer in any period who is limited by space or time—who writes a fiction that, however enlightening for the moment or the region, does not transcend the moment or region—is ultimately the writer who is forgotten. It is for that reason that we find such once great lights as T. S. Stribling—perhaps the most highly praised voice during that short, touted reign of southern realism and satire of the 1920s and early 1930s—altogether forgotten in the late twentieth century, indeed not even attaining that position Robert Penn Warren in 1934 predicted for him: a paragraph in the history of critical realism.[10]

Such is only a *danger* for the contemporary southern writer, not a widespread reality at present. Certain contemporary southern writers, indeed, uphold Davidson's autochthonous ideal to a degree and in a manner he could hardly have imagined—and in a state of innocence that such an ideal was ever pronounced. One would search long and hard to find a writer more devoid of southern self-consciousness than Bobbie Ann Mason (not a New South so much as a No South writer) unless it is, in a very different way, a somewhat older novelist, Cormac McCarthy, whose superbly crafted fiction is often set (as in *The Orchard Keeper*) in a world of pure concreteness and is often, by intent, devoid of any informing point of view at all. A novelist such as Reynolds Price, particularly in his early work, grounds his fiction faithfully in southern social reality without at the same time being at all concerned with his characters *as* Southerners. The *reader* of *A Long and Happy Life* may see Price's characters as "southern," may see his fiction as "southern," as influenced by Welty and Faulkner, but there is very little concern on Price's part as to how his characters fit into the South, what *kind* of Southerners they are, sociologically, historically, geographically. "The South," as an abstraction, an entity, is unimportant, particularly to the early Price.

But I choose to focus, for the remainder of these remarks, on two other contemporary writers who, like Price and McCarthy, are a few years older than those writers who have drawn my attention up until now. Donald Davidson was never much of a kindred spirit with North Carolinians or blacks—the former he roundly indicted as liberals and reformers, the latter he considered racially inferior (or maybe it was the other way around)—but it seems to me that two writers who, in many respects, admirably fulfill Davidson's stated ideal for southern fiction, although not always in the manner he intended—and demonstrate, in a larger sense, the enduring southern concerns for place, nature, community, and the endurance of the past in the present—are the Carolinian Fred Chappell and the black Louisianian Ernest Gaines. Chappell and Gaines—and in Chappell's case I have in mind principally prose works such as *I Am One of You Forever* (1985)—are fully as concerned with traditional southern subjects and themes as were those writers of the Renascence fifty years before. It is perhaps no accident that both come from rich repositories of southern folk culture—Chappell from the southern Appalachians, Gaines from that southern Louisiana mixture of Cajun and Afro-American culture—and neither has shown much interest in the contemporary world of television and shopping malls as most of their contemporaries have.

Davidson would perhaps explain Fred Chappell on the grounds that he was educated at Duke University, not Chapel Hill

—whose "social program," he maintained, had corrupted Thomas Wolfe and other writers. But in fact Chappell (and, for that matter, Wolfe) can hardly be explained principally by where he chose to pursue higher education. He was born and grew up on a farm some fifteen or twenty miles west of Asheville and, as he later wrote, by age fifteen he had long since determined to be a writer. Davidson himself could not have found a more ideal spot for the young writer to be made aware of, at one and the same time, the virtues of an agrarian life and the perils of an industrial one. For a mile or two away from the Chappell farm was the mill town of Canton, home of Champion Paper and Fiber Company, "loud, smoky, noisome," as Chappell later wrote, and creating in the air an awful stink. Chappell describes in an essay, "A Pact with Faustus," his early rebellion against the small town, his coming of age as an artist, his love, in particular, of Thomas Mann's *Doctor Faustus*.[11] One might be reminded of another young Faustus, Wolfe, growing up twenty miles away and thirty-five years before —except that Wolfe's early experience was essentially urban, or at least boom-town southern, and characterized by family disintegration and fragmentation, while Chappell's was essentially rural and stable. Like Wolfe, however, Chappell quickly made his mark as a novelist, with the publication of *It Is Time, Lord* (1963) when he was twenty-seven. After that he made his reputation principally as a poet, particularly in *Midquest* (1981), his long series of narrative poems, many dealing with his family and acquaintances in the mountains (although such a description hardly does justice to their range and complexity). He shared, with John Ashberry, the Bollingen Prize in poetry for 1985.

Yet his novel *I Am One of You Forever* is in some respects his most moving work, his most extensive characterization, Dabney Stuart writes, "of a farm family's cohesion and support."[12] A short book, fewer than two hundred pages, it strikes one in many ways as less novel than memoir, a work which might in fact be placed in that rich but generally neglected tradition of 1940s and 1950s southern memoirs. I think of such works as William Alexander Percy's *Lanterns on the Levee* (1941), James Agee's semi-autobiographical novel *A Death in the Family* (1957), and the work Chappell's most resembles in tone and voice, Ben Robertson's *Red Hills and Cotton* (1942)—another upcountry Carolina farm and family reminiscence (though South Carolina in this case), a lyrical and moving but now nearly forgotten book. Chappell, as Agee, writes fiction, of course, not memoir strictly speaking, but it is semi-autobiographical fiction: the first-person account of a young boy, Jess, growing up in the early 1940s on a mountain farm near a paper mill, outside a town which resembles Canton. At first appearance there is more than a little of Earl Hamner's television "Waltons" in all this—the mountain farm, the close family, the pranks, the bookish budding young writer-narrator. But as one continues there is both less and more than that—less sentimentality and a deeper sense of the fragility of human life, the vanity of human wishes. One finds vivid portraits of Jess's father, a good-humored prankster and fellow conspirator against order and civility (far more scheming than his son) but also a man touched by the vagaries of human existence; of Johnson Gibbs, the orphan who comes to live with Jess's family before going off to meet his death in a training accident at Fort Bragg; of Jess's grandmother, who appears altogether unremarkable to him until he learns that she possesses a sadness occasioned by the missed life, a career in music she might have had if her strict, religious father had not prevented it; of Jess himself, still another version of Huck Finn, playing Huck, that is, to his father's Tom Sawyer, going along with his father's pranks but rarely initiating them; and any number of eccentrics, grotesques, usually relatives. It is these extended family members, Jess's crazy uncles, who provide a rich source of myth and legend, the anecdotal material of everyday life that Bobbie Ann Mason's characters have to acquire, in a thinner form, from television. Uncle Luden the drunken womanizer, Uncle Gurton with his endless beard, Uncle Zeno the storyteller, and Uncle Runkin who brings his coffin to sleep in when he comes to visit: all are nearly larger-than-life characters whose exploits provide constant fascination for young Jess. There is, as well, mystery and transcendence in this book, not in any orthodox religious sense but in a constant presence of the supernatural which captures the imagination of the young narrator.

There could hardly be a better example of the traditional southern novel, with its vivid depiction of place, its reverence for nature, family, community, its nearly purely concrete vision, its portrait of an organic society producing its own mythology. Neither could there be a better example of Davidson's autochthonous ideal, even among the Agrarians and their followers. Chappell's narrator tells his story without a hint of regional self-consciousness, with no discussion whatever of how these mountain people fit into the South or into the national picture, what they represent sociologically, historically, anthropologically. The word *Appalachian* never appears. One finds here a triumph of tone, of point of view. Chappell is concerned solely with the individual drama, with what can be seen and understood from the boy's point of view. The story is obviously being told long after the fact, presumably in the 1980s, but only rarely is there an implied authorial presence, the point of view of the older man looking back (although the language is occasionally that of the older man). Virtually the only time in the novel the implied distance between past and present is stated is in the final sentence of the penultimate chapter: "I couldn't sing then, and I can't sing now. If I could sing—sing, I mean, so that another human being could bear to hear me—I wouldn't sit scribbling this story of long ago time."[13] Aside from rare occurrences such as this, the story is centered altogether in the boy's consciousness, we are immersed in the boy's world, and there is no overt reminder of the passage of time (as there is, for example, in other first-person retrospective narratives such as Allen Tate's *The Fathers* or Peter Taylor's *A Summons to Memphis*), no point of reference other than that of the young boy. Even history—the past—is abstract, thus meaningless to Jess unless it is *his* history, his family. In one of the few hints of a world extending beyond his family and community, he remarks, "Those mountain people of used-to-be seemed as alien to me as Siberians" (p. 39).

I Am One of You Forever is a work, as well, in another southern literary tradition—southwest or frontier humor. Boasting, tall tales, stories within stories, a kind of rough, physical, at times cruel humor—putting Feenamint in Johnson Gibbs's chewing gum, even a story about a powerful bear that kept tearing down fences and, for a time, could not be killed—all are reminiscent of the earlier southern humor of Mark Twain and William Faulkner. Johnson Gibbs exaggerates his pitching prowess in the manner of one of Twain's keelboatmen in *Life on the Mississippi:* "They never got good wood on me and only bad wood when I wanted to give my fielders something to do. I had them looking every place but where the ball was. I had them hypnotized, hornswoggled, and hooligated. They prayed rain on when I was going to pitch and I prayed it off again" (p. 16). And when Johnson is caught in the lie over his baseball exploits, he invents another: "Now what I'm really good at is trout-fishing. With a fly rod. I can pull trout out of the sand and the dry rocks" (p. 21). Even more than Gibbs, Jess's Uncle Zeno is a first-rate yarn spinner, telling stories with the deadpan earnestness of Mark Twain's Simon Wheeler ("He never smiled, he rarely frowned . . . he never betrayed the slightest suspicion of enthusiasm," Twain writes) in "The Notorious Jumping Frog of Calaveras County":[14]

> Dry, flat, almost without inflection, [Uncle Zeno] delivered those stories with the mechanical precision of an ant toting a bit of leaf mold to its burrow. Yet Uncle Zeno had no discernible purpose in telling his stories, and there was little arrangement in the telling. . . . And he took no interest in our reactions. If the story was funny our laughter made no more impression upon him than a distant butterfly; when we were downcast at a sad story, he did not seem to realize it. His attention was fixed elsewhere. [pp. 97–98]

"That puts me in mind of," he customarily begins, and holds forth until his muse departs.

But Jess the narrator, Chappell the author, not only repeats the tall tales of others, he tells any number himself—like Uncle Zeno, utterly serious, passing it all on as truth. Jess and his father have a great desire to see the end of Uncle Gurton's beard, a marvel forty years in the making which he keeps tucked in his overalls bib. They get a sleeping draught from the veterinarian and put it in his buttermilk, then go up to his room after he is asleep, unhook the overalls and find a "creeklet of shining white" (p. 57). They find, indeed, that the beard never ends: "Billow on billow of gleaming dry wavy silver beard, spilling out over the sheet and spreading over the bed like an overturned bucket of milk. It flowed over the foot of the bed and then down the sides, noiseless, hypnotic. . . . The flow of beard was up to my calves now. . . . Over the bed the beard had climbed until it was like a fogbank, only more solid." Jess then sees a mermaid climbing out of the beard, then "a damn big white whale," and the beard pushes into the hall, down the steps, and fills the entire house (pp. 58–59).

Jess explains no further. Tall tale or parable—concerning the wages of those whose curiosity brings them to violate the privacy of another human creature—there is nothing in the telling that suggests that this is much more remarkable to Jess than other of his experiences. All of life is extraordinary to the child's imagination, and this is hardly the only time that the supernatural is reported with little more amazement than the natural. We witness a telegram that, when set afire, will not burn: the telegram brings news of Johnson Gibbs's death in training camp, and over the weeks it performs marvellous maneuvers—changes size and shape, appears and disappears—but like Dick Allbright's baby in the barrel in Twain's tall tale in *Life on the Mississippi,* it will not disappear. The telegram is, among other things, a metaphor for grief: it will not disappear because the beholders refuse to come to terms with the news it contains.

Jess accepts all—the critical vision is nearly alien to him—but the supernatural event that moves him most profoundly is the storm that he, his father, and Johnson witness. It is a storm unlike any other, one which first appears to take Johnson into itself ("he was some part of the storm now . . . Johnson was another kind of presence than a man") and one whose lightning lands in a hole just in front of them:

> It was a broad round shaft like a great radiant auger, boring into cloud and mud at once. Burning. Transparent. And inside this cylinder of white-purple light swam shoals of creatures we could never have imagined. . . .
>
> They were storm angels. Or maybe they were natural creatures, whose natural element was storm, as the sea is natural to the squid and shark. . . .
>
> This tower of energies went away then, and there was another thrust of lightning just outside the wall. It was a less impressive display, just an ordinary lightning stroke, but it lifted the three of us thrashing in midair for a long mo-

> ment, then dropped us breathless and sightless on the damp ground. We crawled toward one another and clung together like men overboard in heavy seas. We were bewildered and frightened not by the nearness of death but by the nearness of life. [pp. 71–72]

It is the nearness of life, particularly of the natural world, its intense sweetness and mystery, that moves Jess deeply but also disturbs him, and never more than in the book's postscript, "Helen." "It seemed that there were four of us in a hunting cabin high on a mountain near the Tennessee border," Jess begins, "Uncle Luden, Johnson Gibbs, my father, and me. And it seemed that it began to snow the second day" (p. 180). What we have, it appears at first, is another in that tradition of southern hunting stories which are more than hunting stories, the initiation story with the older men and the young boy dreaming of killing his first deer—Isaac McCaslin a half-century later not in the Big Woods of Mississippi but in the Great Smokies. And it continues to be that for a time, as Chappell immerses us in this all-male world of rough clothes and food and whiskey and stories and jokes. But this hunting story turns into something quite different: "I began to feel a little as a stranger among them," Jess reports. "They knew different things than I did." After midnight, as the fire sinks to embers and the men go to sleep, Jess lies awake and thinks: "In my mind was the light of summer and its grass smells and sweat and dusty roads. I thought a little why we had come here, what it would be like to kill a deer" (p. 181). And suddenly, as he lies awake, he hears Gibbs, in his sleep, speak the name "Helen," and then, a moment later, Uncle Luden, in *his* sleep, mutter "Helen," and, shortly afterward, his father make the same sound. At the same time, Jess believes (although he reports he does not actually see them) that all three men sit bolt upright in their beds and stare out at a spot in front of the fireplace. Jess looks, too, and beholds "a face . . . , the features blurred by a veil and yet familiar to me, I fancied, if I could remember something long ago and in a distant place." As the face disappears, he realizes that he "was disturbed most of all by the unplaceable familiarity of the vision. Who was this woman with thick black hair and those penetrating brown eyes?" (pp. 182–83). Jess could not remember and he falls asleep.

The possibilities in Jess's vision are endless. If we approach his tale rationally, of course, we conclude that it was *his* dream, not theirs, that it was Jess who envisioned, meditated upon, and thought if not spoke "Helen." And the dream may have extended beyond the vision of Helen. The language in the chapter's beginning—"It seemed that there were four of us in a hunting cabin. . . . it seemed that it began to snow"—is the language of unreality, the language of dreams. It suggests that the entire trip, not just the vision of Helen, might have been a dream. We do not know why the dream took the form it did, and neither does Jess. The men had not been talking about women—Jess had thought it curious that they had not—and nothing in their stories would have led him to contemplate female beauty (although much in his twelve-year-old hormones might have). We might also logically assume that young Jess, as a ranging and romantic reader who had delved into antiquity (elsewhere in the book he mentions Homer and Schliemann) and whose father had told him of the *Iliad*, might well have had Helen of Troy in mind ("a face" he had encountered "long ago and in a distant place"), but if so he does not specifically make the connection, nor—Chappell would say—is it important that we do. What matters is Jess's response to this profoundly disturbing moment in the middle of the night. When he awakens the next morning he finds all the men "open and careless" as before, but "I felt myself at a distance from them, left out" (p. 183). The men pack to leave, the weather having grown too bad to hunt, and as the others move out to the car Jess sits alone in the cabin until Johnson Gibbs returns and, "his voice sound[ing] deep and hollow," asks "Well, Jess, are you one of us or not?" (p. 184).

These are the novel's final words, and it would be partly correct to say that the title of the book answers Johnson's question. But it is more complicated than that. Jess-Chappell is telling this story forty years after the fact, and the title might well be as much desire as affirmation. The boy Jess, even at twelve, is beginning to discover a dual allegiance, a pulling two ways, a devotion to what he has come from but also to the new world he senses he is entering, the world of adult sexuality and of mind and ideas and experiences that will go far beyond the mountain fastness that has been home.

What the young Jess experiences, what Chappell experiences, is what any number of twentieth-century southern writers before him, ranging from the Agrarians to (at least in the latter part of his career) Thomas Wolfe, had found—that no matter how much one wants, at a certain level, one cannot altogether will himself back into the world he came from. That is what the Agrarians tried to do—in any number of ways, among them in the essays they wrote for *I'll Take My Stand*—but they could not because, for a time, they had assumed a critical distance and, beyond that, had become citizens of a larger world of the imagination. That is also what Wolfe tried to do—and his lack of success is suggested by the title of his posthumous novel, *You Can't Go Home Again.* That is precisely what Chappell attempts in his book as well—to will himself back—but he too, at the time he writes, has become a citizen of that larger world, and neither can he go back all the way. The title of Wolfe's final novel might be, in a sense too painful to acknowledge, the title of his own.

2

I shift not only writers but locales at this point; and one can hardly find in the American South a greater distance, in any number of ways, than that between a snowed-in cabin in the Smokies and the quarters of a plantation in steamy Louisiana Cajun country. But Ernest Gaines, like Fred Chappell, is a contemporary southern writer in his mid-fifties who grounds his work in a rich and full folk culture and places great value on those concerns—place, community, man's ties to the natural world—which have long been at the center of the southern literary imagination. Indeed, it would be difficult to find in contemporary southern letters any writer who is more traditional, in the best sense of that word, than Gaines—not only, as I have already said, in his attention to place and community but also in his deep sense of the elemental, his distrust of abstraction, his awareness of the past in the present, and his continued attention to that most frequently treated and most dramatically powerful of southern subjects, racial tension and conflict. At a time when most white southern novelists have left racial themes nearly behind—they can well afford to—Gaines still grounds his fiction in racial conflict, courage, endurance. He knows well that race did not disappear as a fact of southern life and a source of rich drama when, after 1970, Dixie moved into the sun.

And Gaines is not alone among contemporary black writers who, taken as a whole, tend to be more concerned with community, place, and the past and its legacy—and to ground their fiction more fully in a rich traditional folk culture—than do most of their white counterparts. It is an irony a hidebound Agrarian like Donald Davidson would find difficult to accept, although it is really not an irony at all, since the black Southerner *always* had these concerns and the rich black culture was always there to be seen if Davidson and the Agrarians had noticed. In any case, it is in Afro-American writers such as Gaines and Alice Walker—and to name two Southerners by legacy and interest if not by birth, Toni Morrison and Gloria Naylor—that we find much of the old power of southern fiction. Few black writers produce minimalist fiction; few black writers set their work in a world whose boundaries are established by popular culture, few take their mythology from television and film, few are content with portraying a middle-class consumer existence. Such is to generalize and to overstate the point, but it might be argued that Afro-American fiction, within contemporary southern literature, is what, in the 1930s, 1940s, and 1950s, white southern fiction was within the national literature—a powerful, folk-based, past-conscious, often mythic expression of a storytelling culture within a larger literature.

There are exceptions, of course, on both sides, exceptions to the assumption that the contemporary black writer values folk culture and affirms place and community more than the contemporary white southern writer. As we have seen, Lee Smith and Fred Chappell, among other writers, place great value on place and community, and, among black writers, one finds neither place nor community in the superbly talented nearly postmodern short-story writer James Alan McPherson, originally of Georgia. McPherson's protagonists are often rootless, living in a fragmented world; if community comes into play at all, it often—as in McPherson's story "The Silver Bullet"—is nearly parodied. One finds certain younger black Southerners, like John Holman, as addicted to malls and VCRs and contemporary mass culture as their white contemporaries, and evincing relatively little racial self-consciousness. And even Alice Walker who, in her book of essays *In Search of Our Mothers' Gardens* (1983), speaks of the sustaining power of the black community with the black church at its center—and proclaims that "what the black Southern writer inherits as a natural right is a sense of *community*" [Walker's italics][15]—in fact in her novels often portrays that traditional black community in an unfavorable light. In her early novel *The Third Life of Grange Copeland* (1970), we find a violent, fragmented existence, a legacy of the world that slavery made—closer to the idea of community, or noncommunity, in Richard Wright's *Black Boy* than to Walker's own stated ideal of community. We find very little nurturing and sustaining; rather community, when it is acknowledged at all, is described as a "pious, scorekeeping" sort of thing. We find an even more dismal idea of traditional community in *The Color Purple*, save to the extent to which women band together (even more strongly than in Jill McCorkle's *Tending to Virginia*) to create their own caring, nurturing community.

But all of this moves away from Ernest Gaines, and it is Gaines's work to which I want to return. For it is Gaines more than any other black Southerner who realizes in his fiction most of those qualities I have mentioned that were long assumed to be the domain of the white southern writer. Indeed, it is not overstating the case to contend that Gaines, in most respects, admirably fulfills Davidson's autochthonous ideal. Such at first appearance would hardly seem to be the case—since, to Davidson, the writer who was concerned with racial justice was necessarily concerned with "social problems" and thus compromised his art. Nothing, in Gaines's case, could be further from the truth. In *The Autobiography of Miss Jane Pittman* (1971), *A Gathering of Old Men* (1983), and other novels he indeed writes about racial conflict, but he approaches such conflict concretely. We find no editorializing, no special pleading: the story, the individual drama, is all. I want to consider, in particular, *A Gathering of Old Men*, the story of some dozen and a half Louisiana black men, mainly over seventy, who come together to protect one of their own, eighty-two-year-old Mathu, who is thought to have shot and killed a race-baiting Cajun. Although the potential for "problem fiction" —social commentary, regional self-consciousness—is implicit in such a story, Gaines resists the temptation. The *reader*, bringing his knowledge of Selma and Oxford and Philadelphia, Mississippi, to the story, may see it as another "southern racial story," he may bring *his* regional consciousness to his reading. But to Gaines this is not documentary, not sociology, not abstraction of any sort. It is rather a story about a group of men interested in righting very personal old scores and affirming personal dignity, little concerned with how they fit into the larger picture. Again, Gaines, the literary artist, is concerned only with the individual drama being played out on *his* particular postage stamp of native soil in southern Louisiana.

If this sounds like Faulkner, it is for good reason. For of all the contemporary southern writers—Styron, Price, and Cormac McCarthy among them—who at one time or another have been compared to Faulkner, none except perhaps Styron resembles Faulkner so much as Gaines, at his best, does. As much as any southern writer since Faulkner, Gaines has appropriated a particular limited territory in the southern provinces, has set most of his fiction there and made it his own. In *The Autobiography of Miss Jane Pittman, A Gathering of Old Men,* and other novels we come to know the area thirty or forty miles north and west of Baton Rouge—the cane fields, the swamps, the quarters, the fictional town of Bayonne (Gaines's equivalent to Faulkner's Jefferson)—as intimately as we know Faulkner's Yoknapatawpha. With Gaines one returns as well to the ambitious undertaking, the moral seriousness of a fiction involving racial conflict, the forces of history being reflected in a particular human drama—a particular drama of universal meaning—all of which we have in Faulkner. The conflict in Gaines is more complicated than black versus white, since whites are divided into Anglos and Cajuns (as, indeed, in Faulkner's fiction about earliest Mississippi, one finds three coexisting and competing cultures, white, black, and red). But it is Gaines's *manner* of handling racial conflict that most resembles Faulkner's—in *A Gathering of Old Men,* for example, with a great tolerance and understanding, not anger or bitterness or vengeance, portraying Cajun characters as sensitively as he portrays black ones, realizing that the hot-blooded Cajun who was shot and killed suffered from a similar inferiority to the landowning whites of English descent who viewed both blacks and Cajuns as if they were, in the words of the slain man's brother, "a breed below you."[16]

Gaines shares with Faulkner, as well, a valuing of the old ways, even a basic conservatism in matters other than racial change. The old men who gather in Marshall's Quarters deeply regret the passing of most of the old ways, preferring mules and plows and hoes to tractors, indeed fearing the tractors which have put some of them out of work, which, in the words of old Johnny Paul, threaten even the graveyard where his ancestors lie: "I was scared . . . one day that tractor was go'n come in there and plow up them graves, getting rid of all proof that we ever was" (p. 92). As the men gather with their twelve-gauge shotguns to defend old Mathu, the body of Beau Boutan lying nearby, not far away is Beau's tractor, still running until the sheriff arrives two or three hours later and has his deputy cut it off—the machine in the garden, in this slave-made sugarcane plantation that these descendants of slaves nonetheless see as a garden.

We find in *A Gathering of Old Men* any number of other parallels to Faulkner, although that is not to say that Gaines is derivative—save perhaps in narrative technique, employing multiple narrators somewhat in the manner of *As I Lay Dying,* although not so successfully as Faulkner. In other respects, it is simply that Gaines, for whatever reasons of temperament, experience, and background, possesses an artistic vision which, though falling short in tragic power and sheer verbal virtuosity, resembles Faulkner's in many respects. There is the Faulknerian fusion of the grave and the comic, a certain hilarity in the midst of violence and suffering. One considers the shootout at the end, the resulting confusion, the plight of the beefy white Sheriff Mapes who is downed with a bullet in the arm and strives mightily but unsuccessfully to get up: the pace, the tone, the comic context are reminiscent of the section of Faulkner's "Spotted Horses" in which the horses break loose, causing chaos and bodily injury.

One finds characters in abundance who would be at home in Faulkner's Yoknapatawpha: Mathu, the proud, unyielding black man, an older version of Lucas Beauchamp; Jack Marshall, the weary aristocrat reminiscent of Mr. Compson, alcoholic, burdened, and ready to give up; the self-important but completely ineffectual deputy sheriff; the well-meaning, frightened, and ultimately pathetic barkeeper, Tee Jack, whose first-person section is one of the narrative triumphs of the book; and, finally, the sheriff, Mapes, who develops from the stereotype of the racist, abusive white southern lawman into a more complex figure—plain white, in his late sixties, intent on fairness as he sees it, conditioned by his society just as fully as Beau Boutan is by his. What emerges, at last, is indeed a sympathetic, even half-affectionate portrait of this Deep South sheriff who, after all, is one *of* the "old men" who gather—but who wants nothing more than for the standoff to end so he can go fishing. One finally sees Gaines, like Faulkner, as the cosmic overseer of his fictional universe, sympathizing with any number of his characters, black, Cajun, plain white (nearly all except, perhaps, the white planter class) but identifying with none in particular, making, finally, in the midst of chaos and bloodshed, a rather affirmative statement about race—that all these people are victims of a certain conditioning, products of a particular system but, with few exceptions, possessing a certain honor and dignity and sharing far more in common than not.

It would be misleading, however, to stop there, to contend that Gaines is an altogether traditional practitioner of that Faulknerian drama of the human heart in conflict with itself. For there is in Gaines a quality which often, while dealing honestly with place, community, history, and nature, also turns these traditional concerns on themselves. In *A Gathering of Old Men* we find the old southern subject (racial conflict), the old setting (the rural South), the old theme (the power of community)—but all with a difference. We have, at one and the same time, an affirmation of the continuing power of community in southern fiction *and* a reversal of certain traditional assumptions about community. We think of how the community works, for example, in *Light in August*, that classic study of the power of a communal spirit which both embraces and rejects, which takes in kindred spirits *and* creates pariahs, and which, more than anything else, demands a uniformity of thought on the subject of race and creates a climate of opinion and emotion that makes the lynching of Joe Christmas possible, even inevitable. The same has been true in much other southern fiction besides Faulkner, in much southern life beyond literature. Those who have felt most keenly the negative power of white community were black Southerners, whose conduct was prescribed, regulated, and monitored according to the dictates of the southern white power structure; and whose misconduct, in the eyes of the white community, was punished severely, the most severely by lynching.

What we find in *A Gathering of Old Men* is indeed the power of community, then, but it is the power of the black community, not the white, that asserts itself—a power that, rather than condoning and facilitating a lynching, prevents one. The old black men who gather in the quarters challenge, even intimidate, the sheriff, that authority in southern society who usually had *done* the intimidating. The white community at Marshall, by contrast, is broken and powerless. All that remains is Jack Marshall—who escapes by way of alcohol and sleep as the confrontation takes place on his land—his equally oblivious wife, Bea, and their niece Candy, whose most memorable action in the novel is throwing a tantrum at the end because she no longer is heeded by the newly courageous blacks. (Indeed, *A Gathering of Old Men* raises questions of gender as well as race. Women play a secondary role in this novel as in *I Am One of You Forever:* in Chappell, a cautious, conservative check on the romantic yearnings and adventures of males—one is reminded of Faulkner's Mrs. Littlejohn in "Spotted Horses"; in Gaines, well-meaning but finally incompetent, the novel reinforcing gender stereotypes at the same time it destroys racial ones.) If indeed there is any communal solidarity among these Louisiana whites, it resides in the closely knit Cajuns, who meet at the Boutan house and discuss whether to take the law into their own hands and avenge the death of one of their own. Such had always, in the past, been their course of action. Blacks and Cajuns, not the traditional southern community of white Anglo-Saxons (who were, in fact, usually Scots-Irish), hold the power here.

There are several other reversals in Gaines's treatment of community, among them the fact that religion plays no part in *this* black communal spirit, that indeed the only unsympathetic black character in the novel is the cowardly preacher, Jameson, who commands respect from neither black nor white. But I wanted to turn finally to another aspect of Gaines's novel which seems to me to relate to the subject of community, place, traditional culture, and the modern world. For although the world Gaines gives us in *A Gathering of Old Men* is the rural world of traditional southern fiction, his story is *set* in the late 1970s, and not even black and Cajun Louisiana in 1979 was immune to contemporary mass culture. In Louisiana, on a sunny autumn weekend, mass culture means most of all football. It seems that Beau Boutan's brother, Gilbert, is a star LSU fullback who teams with a black running back—together the press has labeled them Salt and Pepper—and when Gil is summoned home from Baton Rouge on a Friday afternoon, just before the Ole Miss game, to consult with his father and brothers as to when and how they will exact revenge, Gil refuses to go along; and since he will not ride with his brothers and friends, his father calls off the lynching party. It would be nice to think that Gil's courage, his moral indignation, his regard for Pepper prevents a lynching, but in fact it is something quite other than that: it is the power of public relations. For Gil is being touted for national honors and, as he tells his father, "I couldn't make All-American, Papa, if I was involved in something against the law" (p. 138). Gone, then, is the old integrity of revenge. "The day when family responsibility is put aside for a football game," his father exclaims, unbelieving (p. 143). "Go run the ball. Let it take the place of family" (p. 146).

The reader, of course, is left with ambivalence, particularly since Gaines makes the revenge-minded father as sympathetic as his peace-seeking son. Who can be deeply moved when it is not moral outrage at all but rather high-priced, high-tech, and high-visibility LSU football that makes revenge impossible? It does give some support to the argument that Bear Bryant and his recruitment of black athletes did more for race relations in the Deep South than any politician could ever do—or, to put it another way, if you couldn't legislate morality, you could bring it about on a football field. But it also leaves one with doubts about all those lofty abstractions applied to and by white Southerners who, after 1970, were going to wipe out racism because of a renewed attention to the better angels of their nature. The incident of Gil Boutan, I suppose, is more truthful than we might like to think: it announces a South that has indeed changed but not always for the noblest of reasons.

Ernest Gaines, of course, has benefited from that change, whatever its reasons (and I do not mean to suggest that all the reasons were self-serving). Indeed, until the last decade or two, Gaines would not likely have been included in a discussion of this sort on "southern writers," despite the fact that, as C. Vann

Woodward once wrote, the black Southerner was the quintessential Southerner.[17] The black Southerner was also, one might add, the quintessential southern *agrarian*, in that he had a closer acquaintance with the soil—a deeper intimacy with it because of working it—than most of the upper-case Agrarians ever had. And finally, for certain reasons I have suggested, the black Southerner might be seen as the quintessential southern *writer*—with his emphasis on family and community, his essentially concrete vision, his feeling for place, *his* legacy of failure, poverty, defeat, and those other well-known qualities of the southern experience, *his* immersion in history and what it produced. Any writer with those qualities and that legacy would seem to be, in many respects, the truest contemporary heir to the southern literary tradition—although such would be, in the eyes of Donald Davidson who helped to define that tradition, a final irony of southern history.

Notes

■

1 THE CONTEMPORARY SOUTHERN WRITER AND THE TRADITION

1. Donald Davidson, *Southern Writers in the Modern World* (Athens: University of Georgia Press, 1958).
2. C. Vann Woodward, "The Irony of Southern History," in *Southern Renascence: The Literature of the Modern South*, ed. Louis D. Rubin, Jr., and Robert D. Jacobs (Baltimore: Johns Hopkins University Press, 1953), 63–79; and William Faulkner, *Absalom, Absalom!* (1936; reprint, New York: Vintage Books, 1972), 361.
3. Richard Weaver, "Aspects of the Southern Philosophy," in *Southern Renascence*, ed. Rubin and Jacobs, 28; Allen Tate, "The New Provincialism," *Virginia Quarterly Review* 21 (1945), esp. 270–72; and Louis D. Rubin, Jr., "Fugitives as Agrarians: The Impulse Behind *I'll Take My Stand*," in *William Elliott Shoots a Bear: Essays on the Southern Literary Imagination* (Baton Rouge: Louisiana State University Press, 1975), 145–63.
4. See Weaver, "Aspects of the Southern Philosophy," 14–30, and Robert B. Heilman, "The Southern Temper," in *Southern Renascence*, ed. Rubin and Jacobs, 3–13.
5. Louis D. Rubin, Jr., "William Styron: Notes on a Southern Writer in Our Time," in *Writers of the Modern South: The Faraway Country* (Seattle: University of Washington Press, 1963), 185–230.

6. Gerald W. Johnson, "The Horrible South," in *South-Watching: Selected Essays by Gerald W. Johnson*, ed. Fred Hobson (Chapel Hill: University of North Carolina Press, 1983), 37.
7. Julius Rowan Raper, "Inventing Modern Southern Fiction: A Post-modern View," forthcoming in *Southern Literary Journal*. For excellent studies of certain southern fiction writers since World War II —but before the 1980s—see also Walter Sullivan, *Requiem for the Renascence: The State of Fiction in the Modern South* (Athens: University of Georgia Press, 1976); Lewis A. Lawson, *Another Generation: Southern Fiction Since World War II* (Jackson: University Press of Mississippi, 1984); and George Core, ed., *Southern Fiction Today: Renascence and Beyond* (Athens: University of Georgia Press, 1969).

2 A QUESTION OF CULTURE—AND HISTORY

1. Bobbie Ann Mason, *In Country* (New York: Harper and Row, 1985), 23.
2. William Faulkner, Nobel Prize Address, in *The Portable Faulkner*, ed. Malcolm Cowley (1946; reprint, New York: Viking, 1966), 724.
3. Allen Tate, "The New Provincialism," *Virginia Quarterly Review* 21 (1945): 272; and William Faulkner, *Requiem for a Nun* (New York: Vintage Books, 1951), 92.
4. See, e.g., Robert Lewis Dabney, *A Defence of Virginia and Through Her of the South* (New York: Hale, 1867). In considering the accounts of Dabney and other Civil War apologists, we should not forget that those who wrote were not representative of all southern points of view. One wonders, despite the glorious reunions and parades and written memoirs, if some ex-Confederates, largely unlettered ones, did not question their lost cause as deeply as the Vietnam vets did theirs. Because they were largely unlettered, we will never fully know.
5. See, for a discussion of Mason and history, Robert H. Brinkmeyer, Jr., "Finding One's History: Bobbie Ann Mason and Contemporary Southern Literature," *Southern Literary Journal* 19 (1987): 20–33.
6. See H. L. Mencken, "The Sahara of the Bozart," in *Prejudices, Second Series* (New York: Knopf, 1920), 134–54; and W. J. Cash, *The Mind of the South* (New York: Knopf, 1941).

7. See Walter Taylor, *Faulkner's Search for a South* (Urbana: University of Illinois Press, 1983), 8; and Allen Tate, *Memoirs and Opinions 1926–1974* (Chicago: Swallow Press, 1975), 7–8.
8. Mervyn Rothstein, "Homegrown Fiction," *New York Times Magazine*, May 15, 1968, p. 101; and William Alexander Percy, *Lanterns on the Levee: Recollections of a Planter's Son* (1941; reprint, Baton Rouge: Louisiana State University Press, 1974), 140.
9. For valuable discussions of Lee Smith, see Anne Goodwyn Jones, "The World of Lee Smith," *Southern Quarterly* 22 (1983): 115–39; and Suzanne W. Jones, "City Folks in Hoot Owl Holler: Narrative Strategy in Lee Smith's *Oral History*," *Southern Literary Journal* 20 (1987): 101–12.
10. Lee Smith, *Oral History* (New York: Ballantine Books, 1983), 1, 2.
11. Walker Percy, "The Loss of the Creature," in *The Message in the Bottle* (New York: Farrar, Straus and Giroux, 1975), 46–53.
12. Larry McMurtry and Benjamin DeMott, excerpts of reviews of *Ray*, in *Ray*, by Barry Hannah (New York: Penguin Books, 1981), i, iii.
13. Barry Hannah, *The Tennis Handsome* (New York: Knopf, 1983), 133.
14. R. Vanarsdall, "The Spirit Will Win Through: An Interview with Barry Hannah," *Southern Review* 19 (1983): 338.
15. Barry Hannah, *Geronimo Rex* (New York: Avon Books, 1972), 216, 217, 218.

3 RICHARD FORD AND JOSEPHINE HUMPHREYS

1. Bruce Weber, "Richard Ford's Uncommon Characters," *New York Times Magazine*, April 10, 1988, pp. 50, 63; and Kay Bonetti, quoting Ford, in "An Interview with Richard Ford," *Missouri Review* 10 (1987): 71.
2. Richard Ford, "My Mother, in Memory," *Harper's* 275 (1987): 44.
3. Richard Ford, "The Three Kings," *Esquire* 100 (1983): 581.
4. Richard Ford, *The Sportswriter* (New York: Vintage Books, 1986), 24, 144.
5. One might contend, of course, that the items in mail-order catalogs are *not* the things themselves, but rather representations, abstractions.

   As concerns Frank's viewing of Johnny Carson—which he shares with Mason's Sam Hughes, among others—it is perhaps worthy of mention that in contemporary southern fiction Johnny Carson and Ed McMahon seem to be heeded, pondered, and quoted far more than Robert E. Lee and William Faulkner.

6. William Faulkner, *Absalom, Absalom!* (1936; reprint, New York: Vintage Books, 1972).
7. One should probably draw the line, however, at claiming kin for Eugene Gant's Uncle Bascom Pentland in Thomas Wolfe's *Of Time and the River*—another questing expatriate Southerner in the Northeast.
8. In most of his work Ford demonstrates a sensitivity to place, even in a work so apparently rootless as *Rock Springs*, the first two stories of which, "Rock Springs" and "Great Falls," are not only connected to but named for place. In another story in that collection, "The Children," the narrator, looking back at his teens in northern Montana, considers that it was "the place itself, as much as the time in our lives or our characters, that took part in the small things that happened and made them memorable" (p. 70).

   Ford is hardly the only expatriate southern writer who cannot escape a fascination with place. It is hard to find a contemporary novel more concerned with place, for example (as well as family, time, and community), than Gail Godwin's *The Finishing School*, which is set in upstate New York.
9. The town of Haddam, Ford writes, is a place "where it is not at all hard for a literalist to contemplate the world" (p. 48). Whether the founder of Haddam was, in fact, named *Wallace* Haddam, as Frank tells us he was, I have not been able to ascertain, but Ford's brief description of the town includes references to Wallace Haddam, Wallace Hill, and insurance brokers. Perhaps one can avoid thinking of Wallace Stevens, but given Ford's sly and allusive manner it is not easy.
10. Herman Melville, *Moby Dick* (1851; reprint, Signet Books, 1961), 536; *New York Magazine*, quoted inside cover of *The Sportswriter*.
11. Robert Penn Warren, *All the King's Men* (1946; reprint, Bantam Books, 1959), 309.
12. Ford also shares with Percy a penchant for striking similes. His "dumb as a cashew," "dreamy as Tarzan," "dangerous as a snake,"

"distracted as a camel," "apprehensive as a pilgrim," and so on surpass—to choose just a couple of many in Percy's *The Last Gentleman*—"sweating like a field horse" or "life [which] seems as elegant as algebra."

13. Bob Summer, "Josephine Humphreys," *Publisher's Weekly*, September 4, 1987, pp. 49–50. See also, on Humphreys and Charleston, Josephine Humphreys, "My Real Invisible Self," in *A World Unsuspected: Portraits of Southern Childhood*, ed. Alex Harris (Chapel Hill: University of North Carolina Press, 1987). *A World Unsuspected* contains autobiographical childhood portraits of Bobbie Ann Mason, James Alan McPherson, Barry Hannah, and other contemporary writers, as well as Humphreys.
14. Josephine Humphreys, *Dreams of Sleep* (New York: Penguin Books, 1984), 56, 162.
15. Walker Percy, *Love in the Ruins* (New York: Farrar, Straus and Giroux, 1971), 219, and *The Last Gentleman* (New York: Farrar, Straus and Giroux, 1966), 21; and Barry Hannah, *Ray* (New York: Penguin Books, 1981), 44–46. One also finds gentle digs at Ohioans in Percy's *The Moviegoer* and *Lancelot*.
16. Ann Hulbert, "All in the Family," *New Republic*, December 24, 1984, p. 38.
17. For a discussion of rotation and repetition in Percy's fiction, see Martin Luschei, *The Sovereign Wayfarer: Walker Percy's Diagnosis of the Malaise* (Baton Rouge: Louisiana State University Press, 1972), 44–52, and Linda Whitney Hobson, *Understanding Walker Percy* (Columbia: University of South Carolina Press, 1988), 15–20 and 33–41.
18. Humphreys might well have chosen Will's name for something of the same reason Walker Percy named his protagonist in *The Last Gentleman* Will Barrett (will bear it, will endure it), although she does not press the issue. In fact, it is not Will Barrett whom Will Reese resembles so much as, biographically at least, the young Percy himself—who also left his Deep South home to attend Chapel Hill, who spent *his* time there reading fiction and poetry but majoring in pre-med, who also became a physician (in Percy's case, a nonpracticing one), and also returned to the Deep South to meditate on sadness and loss.

19. Michael Griffith, "Josephine Humphreys's *Dreams of Sleep* and the New Domestic Novel." I am grateful to Mr. Griffith for sharing this unpublished paper with me.

4 CONTEMPORARY SOUTHERN FICTION AND THE AUTOCHTHONOUS IDEAL

1. George B. Tindall, "The Significance of Howard W. Odum to Southern History: A Preliminary Estimate," *Journal of Southern History* 24 (1958): 285–307.
2. I have written hardly at all, of course, of those contemporary southern writers who began to publish as early as the 1940s and 1950s but who produced some of their best fiction in the 1980s—Peter Taylor, Elizabeth Spencer, Doris Betts, and Reynolds Price, among them. These writers—in novels such as *A Summons to Memphis* (1986), *The Salt Line* (1984), *Heading West* (1981), and Price's *Kate Vaiden* (1986) and *Good Hearts* (1988)—combine a sense of tradition with a keen understanding of the contemporary South. The southern past, even the recent past, is far from glorified. As one of Spencer's characters says, "The past is quicksand" (*The Salt Line*, p. 138). But the present may be even worse if we are to judge by Price's *Good Hearts*, which brings Rosacoke and Wesley of *A Long and Happy Life* up to 1986—a dismal picture of life in the Sun Belt, even in booming Raleigh, that city Rand-McNally named in the mid-eighties as one of the three best places to live in the United States.
3. Just what is southern and what is not, which writers are southern and which are not, is a continuing problem for the student of southern literature. One thinks of Jayne Anne Phillips, author of *Machine Dreams* and *Black Tickets*, a writer generally designated "southern." But Phillips was born and grew up in northeastern West Virginia, was educated in Morgantown (much closer to Pittsburgh than anything southern), and writes about an area that has more in common with Pennsylvania than, say, Virginia.

   As concerns Anne Tyler's adopted home, one finds in Baltimore evidence for what might be called the Shrinking South. Baltimore was certainly considered a southern city in the nineteenth century, and Maryland a southern state. Indeed, Delaware and—around 1800

—even New Jersey were sometimes referred to as "southern." But none would be considered southern now, evidence perhaps not so much of a Shrinking South as of a Slipping one—that tendency of the "South" over the past two centuries to slide down the Atlantic seaboard and along the Gulf, to slip both south and west.

4. Anne Tyler, *Dinner at the Homesick Restaurant* (New York: Berkley Books, 1982), 291–92, 222.
5. Linda Wagner-Martin, " 'Just the doing of it': Southern Women Writers and the Idea of Community," forthcoming in *Southern Literary Journal.*
6. Bobbie Ann Mason, "Drawing Names," in *Shiloh and Other Stories* (New York: Harper and Row, 1982), 104. Iris's husband explains her remark: "She gets that from television." I have already remarked on the importance of television in Mason's fiction. One might examine its importance in Jill McCorkle's as well. For example, in *The Cheer Leader,* Jo Spencer is just as devoted to *The Andy Griffith Show* as Mason's Sam Hughes is to *M*A*S*H* and Johnny Carson; if we measure a character's commitment to traditional values by the television shows she can't miss, I suppose this makes Jo more traditional than Sam. And when characters in contemporary southern fiction want a basis of comparison for real-life drama, they hardly say any more (as does Shreve to Quentin in *Absalom, Absalom!*) "It's better than Ben Hur!" Rather (like Ginny in *Tending to Virginia*), "[It's] better than a soap opera" (p. 233).
7. Jill McCorkle, *The Cheer Leader* (Chapel Hill, N.C.: Algonquin, 1984), 53.
8. See, e.g., Davidson's essays "The Southern Poet and His Tradition," *Poetry* 40 (1932): 94–103; and "The Trend of Literature," in *Culture in the South,* ed. W. T. Couch (Chapel Hill: University of North Carolina Press, 1934).
9. Donald Davidson, "The Artist as Southerner," *Saturday Review,* May 15, 1926, p. 782.
10. Robert Penn Warren, "T. S. Stribling: A Paragraph in the History of Critical Realism," *American Review* 2 (1934): 463–86.
11. Fred Chappell, "A Pact with Faustus," in *The Fred Chappell Reader* (New York: St. Martin's Press, 1987), 479–90.
12. Dabney Stuart, " 'What's Artichokes?': An Introduction to the Work of Fred Chappell," in *The Fred Chappell Reader,* xiv.

13. Fred Chappell, *I Am One of You Forever* (Baton Rouge: Louisiana State University Press, 1985), 179.
14. See Mark Twain, *Life on the Mississippi* (1880; reprint, New York: Hill and Wang, 1961), 15–16; and "The Notorious Jumping Frog of Calaveras County," in *The Complete Short Stories of Mark Twain*, ed. Charles Neider (New York: Hanover House, 1957), 1.
15. Alice Walker, *In Search of Our Mothers' Gardens* (San Diego: Harcourt, Brace, Jovanovich, 1983), 17.
16. Ernest Gaines, *A Gathering of Old Men* (New York: Knopf, 1983), 122.
17. C. Vann Woodward, *American Counterpoint: Slavery and Racism in the North-South Dialogue* (Boston: Little, Brown, 1971), 6.

Index

■

128865